PAPER

AIRPLANE

BROKEN

BONES

Willow
River
Press

Willow River Press
Between the Lines Publishing
1769 Lexington Ave North #286
Roseville MN 55113
btwnthelines.com

First Published: March 2025

Willow River Press is an imprint of Between the Lines Publishing. The Liminal Books name and logo are trademarks of Between the Lines Publishing.

ISBN: (paperback) 978-1-965059-26-5

ISBN: (eBook) 978-1-965059-27-2

PAPER

AIRPLANE

BROKEN

BONES

R.B. Shifman

To those who have been unjustly detained and abused

1980

1980

Shpresa

Ludes

I imagined Shpresa Sula returned to me as a miniature transmogrified version of herself, like a small stuffed monkey clinging to my upper back, the creature's furry mouth whispering secrets from the great beyond into my ear. She didn't speak to me in an actual voice I could hear, but rather, she visited me with a reflection of her distinctive nasal tone, an echo inside my head that mimicked how she sounded in the days that came before the day-after.

At times, I fantasized that Shpresa's spirit had ridden my shoulders since I was very young, monitoring my successes and failures, sometimes giving me sound advice. So, for example, I pretended Shpresa was present in spring of seventh grade, entreating me to ball myself up and get small as my father repeatedly slapped the top of my head, the body part where bruises failed to blossom. This punishment because I lowered the setting on our home's thermostat two notches to seventy-seven degrees.

I also believed Shpresa watched with innocent curiosity when, on the last day of sixth grade, Annie LeFevre, the fourteen-year-old girl down the street, startlingly presented twelve-year-old me with my first kiss while standing in her grandmother's driveway. I'm certain Shpresa could smell the apple shampoo in the girl's hair same as I did, was amused by the surprising sensuality of the kiss at that tender age—Annie's lips soft and tasting like bubble gum, her mouth open, her warm wet tongue a gentle magical snake coiling around my own, brightening the recesses of my sleepy young mind with a rainbow of fizzy sparkles.

Or, in a quiet moment, I pictured that Shpresa warned me not to put up a struggle when, bicycling home from elementary school in the fifth grade, three scruffy teenagers blocked my path and grabbed my handlebars. They threatened to beat me with a Louisville slugger if I didn't give up my bicycle-lock combination. I did, and a year later my bicycle disappeared from the middle school's bike cage.

Yes, I liked to believe Shpresa's energy, her sonic vibrations, whatever, accompanied me on my everyday travels from a very young age. She must have been with me when all these things happened. Right? Because she was always with me, right? All my life. Right?

No.

That couldn't be.

Shpresa Sula was very much alive back in the fifth, sixth, and seventh grades. She died at the end of the eighth grade as the school days dragged on, only two weeks until summer. She died as the air became thick with prickly moisture, the Fort Lauderdale sun growing hot, hot, hotter until the afternoon rains rumbled in from the Everglades, cooling the day, but only slightly. She left us while summer hid around the corner like a crowd-in-waiting at a surprise party, the school break teasing us with its exhilarating temptations: temperate swimming pools, cold cherry popsicles at Little League games, sandy beach days spent waist-deep in the ocean and spitting salt water at each other, and fireworks lighting up a clear black sky. Shpresa died before these things happened. She died before the good stuff. She was only fourteen, and so was I, when she began her cosmic piggyback ride, depositing stardust on my shoulders for me to brush off into the wastebasket each night.

But first, the day-after, the day defined by what the counselor told us.

Spring – the day-after

The day-after was a tired Monday. School had let out, and nothing much had happened that day or the day before, or so we thought. Information was slow back then; news came on at six in the evening, not before.

Monday's after-school gifted-class session had just begun, and the song, "Magic," by Olivia Newton-John flowed surprisingly clear from the small, black transistor radio on Mr. Morrison's desk. I was wondering why Shpresa wasn't in the class when the school's guidance counselor, her mouth a flat line, entered the room. The classroom hummed with the dissonance of eight students chattering at once, the serene stream of music struggling to poke through the chaos. And yet, despite the din, the counselor closed the door softly behind herself as if she might wake a sleeping infant. As if we children might have been startled by the noise of one door closing on our lives.

Was it bad that I didn't recall the counselor's name? I remembered her as Mrs. White because, why not? Mrs. White, her dark hair slicked back in a tight bun, strode to the front of the room, clasped her hands under her abdomen, and cleared her throat. A large, stiff bow at the top of her cream-colored blouse hugged her neckline. Her burnt-orange wool skirt, the thick fabric all wrong for sticky South Florida, dropped straight down to barely cover her knees, but revealed slender calves I never noticed before as I passed her in the hallways. She mindlessly touched the big bow at the base of her neck as if it could protect her from us kids, buttoned up behind a shield so she could give us the news that contorted her face into a grim, fixed expression.

The music ended abruptly. Mrs. White's statuesque pause siphoned the oxygen from the room, ending our conversation and drawing all eyes to her. That's when she told us. "Class, I have sad news. Very sad news. Shpresa Sula passed away late last night following an automobile accident."

Passed away. As if my buddy leaped somewhere fun. Or got tossed about like a football.

I don't think I felt much within that moment. I imagined myself sitting very still inside an invisible egg surrounding my desk chair, nothing able to puncture my gelatinous, impermeable shell. I didn't even need to breathe inside this cocoon as Mrs. White continued talking. She offered us very few details. It happened Sunday evening. Shpresa was riding in the back of a pickup. The driver was a high schooler. The truck rolled, and my buddy was thrown.

At that moment, I knew deep in my heart that Shpresa died because she was tall and heavy. She wasn't simply big and tall for a fourteen-year-old girl; she was big and tall for anybody. When she and I met two years ago in gifted class as we both entered sixth grade, my friend was already five-seven, several inches taller than me. Two years later, when she came back from summer vacation at the start of eighth grade, I was shocked that Shpresa's eyes met those of our gifted teacher, Mr. Morrison, who stood maybe six feet. I said something to her about how tall she'd gotten, probably a bitingly rude comment knowing me, but she merely laughed good-naturedly, said 'yeah, screw you, Steven,' and socked my arm. Ouch. Then we sat side by side in front of the gifted class's new computer, its bright-green prompt blinking inside its black screen. She seemed to know what to do with the magical box, much more than I did. I didn't have a clue about what made the computer tick or what it was even good for, which made me wonder why I was in the gifted class. Shpresa tapped on the keyboard and mumbled about being able to hang with the high schoolers, whom we passed outside as we arrived for our late session at Oakland Park High School. Our middle school next door was under construction, its roof having collapsed in a rainstorm over the summer of 1979, so we spent our eighth-grade school year mornings watching *The Price Is Right* and *Bonanza*, and our afternoons into the evenings attending middle-school classes in the high school building.

"What's that you said about high schoolers?" I asked her.

She explained that because she was tall, she could pass as a high schooler or even a college student. She claimed, in fact, to have hung out that summer with her older sister and her friends who were all high school juniors. She insisted that she'd snuck into a real disco. I remember being jealous of her; my sister, a sophomore, wanted nothing to do with me.

So, that was it then. Shpresa had been riding in a truck with a bunch of older kids because she was big and because the high schoolers treated her like she was one of them. I wondered, was her older sister in the cab of the truck?

Mrs. White was speaking to me.

"What?"

"I said, you seem to have insight, Steven. What are you feeling about your fr—about Shpresa? It's okay to let us know."

What was I feeling? I didn't know. But I was thinking Shpresa died because she was big and looked older than she was. I was thinking the last time I saw her, Friday at about five o'clock, she asked me to smoke pot with her. As usual, she and I cut through the rock pit on our way home from school. Light gray powder puffed from beneath our sneakers as we walked the gravelly trail carved by the bright yellow CAT bulldozer, which sat silently beside funeral-pyre-sized, grayish-white mounds. I told her no, I didn't want to smoke pot, and with a twitch of the corner of her lips, that was that. We exited the rock pit, and she gave me a quick 'see ya',' turned her back to me, and marched down Twenty-first Avenue toward her neighborhood. I zipped across the street, raced through block-style apartment buildings, and hopped the fence to my neighborhood. Pot? My sister kept pot in one of her knee-high boots in her closet, but Shpresa? I never figured she toked up, and it surprised me. I decided I would ask her about it on Monday. Monday never came.

Mrs. White, waiting for me to answer, looked like she expected me to hand her a birthday present. What did this counselor want from me? I shrugged, and she continued to talk to the muted class, her voice like the droning teacher in *Peanuts*: waah, waah, waah, waah, waah. She came back around to me a second time. "Steven, what do you think?"

What do I think? I think you're calling on me a lot.

My face warmed, and as my cheeks flushed, Shpresa, or what remained of my friend in this world, spoke for the first time into my ear:

Steven! Don't be stupid! She wants to draw out your feelings because you and I were friends, you dummy. Everyone saw how close we were in class. Everyone but you knew I had a crush on you. I thought you were charming. So funny and cute. Ask Amy. She knows.

Whoa. Did somebody just speak to me? Shpresa? Also, crush? What? I cast a sideways glance at Amy Buchanan, two seats over, her scrunched and trembling face red and shiny with tears. How come I wasn't crying like that over Shpresa?

I knew you didn't like me like that, Steven. In lunch, you couldn't take your eyes off Laura Kohler. Skinny, dark-haired Laura with a beach body for days. You like pretty girls your own height, not a six-foot, heavy Albanian girl

6

like me. Don't bother saying you never thought that about me. I can see into your mind now. Like, right now, you're staring a little too long at Mrs. Lebanon's legs, getting yourself bothered about an old lady. She could be thirty-five, Steven. Yuck. Also, I just died. Come on, guy. Do you have the hots for her?

I'll never be able to explain why I immediately accepted that my dead friend was speaking to me from some other spiritual plane, or something like that. I just did. And so, I replied to her in my mind: *No, I don't have the hots for the counselor. Okay, maybe sort of. But, Shpresa, you were my friend. My friend. It was so easy being friends. I guess I could have liked you like that. I never thought about it. How did you die? What happened last night, exactly?*

She met my questions with silence. I assumed she didn't want to talk about the details of her own death.

"Steven? Any insight? You seem to understand these things." For a third time, Mrs. Lebanon and her enormous bow circled back to me. This woman was a dog with a bone, growling and shaking, not letting it go. Unfortunately, I was the bone.

I gave her a small, sideways wag of my head, but inside I was yelling, 'I don't know, leave me alone. Nothing to see here. My dead friend isn't talking to me inside my mind.'

Nothing is weird. Everything is fine. I'm fine.

The next day, in first-period social studies, Dave Mumford told me the guy driving the pickup truck with Shpresa in the open bed had been high on ludes, and he'd fallen asleep at the wheel. Any eighth grader at Oakland Park Middle worth his or her salt knew about ludes, which went by other names: Pills. Downers. Rorer 714. Quaaludes. Some kids romanticized Quaaludes, but not me, especially not after that Monday. What's so great about a drug that makes you fall asleep while driving and kill someone's friend-sister-daughter?

About twenty minutes later as I was doing independent reading in that class, Shpresa started talking to me again. *The guy driving was my sister's boyfriend, and he passed out. The truck hit a median, rolled, and I went flying, Steven. You should have seen me, like a flying squirrel. Can you imagine? I soared toward the asphalt like an airplane made of looseleaf paper and soon-to-be-broken bones. My head cracked open like a ripe melon on the hard black tar. You could see my brain.*

Shhh. Don't whisper horrible stuff like that.

Why was Shpresa telling me these gruesome details?

I didn't know.

But I didn't want to know the gory specifics.

I went on with my life each day following the day-after. I couldn't say for sure if I attended Shpresa's funeral or not, although I must have gone to it because everybody did. It wasn't like she and I had been that close outside of school, though. We didn't hang at each other's house, even though she lived less than a mile away from me. I went to her tiny ranch house once, and she visited my small ranch once, too. One time, over her final summer of 1979, we saw each other at Movie City 11. Bumping into her outside of school brought with it an awkward, wordless tension like we had nothing to say until she punched my upper arm in that familiar way and made me watch her play Space Invaders in the arcade beside the theatre.

So, she wasn't my best friend, and this made it easier, or so I thought, to move on from her death. Except Shpresa, or some small part of her, moved on from her death along with me, accompanying me for several years. Resting on my back. Weightlessly draped over my shoulders. A presence in my auditory canal.

Like a living knapsack.

Or a small stuffed monkey, its long furry arms latched onto my neck.

Or a compact, ghostly version of my once big and tall friend.

Telling me the truth, at least as she saw it. Giving me advice.

Some days, I wished her away. Some days, I was as rude to her as I had been in life.

I never thought I would desperately need her.

But I'm pretty sure I carried her everywhere. Like when a bunch of us headed to Annie LeFevre's house two weeks later at the beginning of the summer. Shpresa was there with me. Telling me what not to do.

If only I'd listened.

Annie's

Summer break, Flag Day 1980

That summer, we often biked to the front of our neighborhood, where a row of small ranch houses faced the long side of an empty, rectangular field. Annie's house was six doors down from the corner and across from the middle of the overgrown grassy area. We hung out inside the girl's stuffy, single-car garage playing ping pong and, by Annie's orders, listening to southern rock on the radio, dealer's choice: Lynyrd Skynyrd, Bob Seger, or Molly Hatchet. Bonus diamond song: "Green Grass and High Tides" by The Outlaws, which, on the rare occasion it played on the radio, caused all activity in the garage to screech to a halt as we sang with all our might and played air guitar along with the extended solo.

It might have been Flag Day, 1980. Mid-June. Three of us guys from our cul-de-sac buried deep within the neighborhood wandered down to the outskirts, the field, and ended up in Annie's garage. The space, cramped like her tiny house, was barely large enough to fit the beat-up ping pong table, with its scratched surface and sagging net. On the driveway, her grandmother's Chevy Impala loomed like a dinosaur, with its massive olive-green body and shabby top, once gleaming white but now a drab gray. Annie, who knew a lot about cars, said the Impala was a model from 1972, the last big thing her grandmother ever bought.

Annie rarely played ping pong with us, preferring instead to sit in the cat bird's seat in a mustard-brown tweed lounger chair by the back door of the garage. She kept her legs extended, forcing us to leap over her shins when a perfectly slapped long ball backed us way up. This happened all the time, even though the other side of the table was flush with the front edge of the garage.

We only played singles; there was no room for doubles. So, when we arrived at Annie's, we played rock-paper-scissors to see which of us would play first, and then rock-paper-scissors again to decide who would claim the advantageous spot at the front of the garage. Peter and I played first, and even though I took the coveted side at the front, he beat me 21–18. I was a decent enough player, but Peter and Billy, both baseball players, were more athletic than me, both a smidge quicker and more agile. It was a red-letter day when I beat one of them at any sport. Then Billy beat Peter 26–24, and I came in again. The loser always took the back spot, so I became Annie's victim during my second game; more than once I hopped over her slim, tanned legs, which she stretched close together, wiggling her pink-painted toenails as if to taunt me.

After I hopped over her legs for the third time, I held the ball and shot her the dirtiest look possible, my brows as low as I could get them. She stared at me with an open face, flicking the ash of her cigarette into a misshapen, black clay tray, and swirling a lock of her golden-brown hair behind her ear with her pinky. "What?"

"Stevie! Serve!" Billy, a lanky shirtless silhouette beneath the blazing sun at the front end of the garage, yelled at me.

"What?" she repeated. "You got yer panties in a bunch, pussy? Quit eyeballin' me."

Peter sat on a bar stool at mid-table, against the side of the garage. "Don't worry about Stevie. He needs to get laid."

I sighed. With these guys, it always came back to that. Some days, I felt like maybe the best way to deal with them would be to disappear inside my house for a while like our friend Rob did. "It's just—could you sit cross-legged maybe? Sooner or later, I'm gonna bang your shins." I waved my paddle, its pinkish-red rubber flaking from one corner, at her golden legs.

She blew a stream of smoke above her head. "But you ain't hit 'em yet, so quit yer bellyaching. Win a game, and you got no troubles."

"Steve! Serve!" cried Billy, a boy of few words.

Annie and I faced off for another quiet moment. "And quit looking at my tits while yer at it." She adjusted her beige bra, the straps peeking from beneath her yellow tank top. "I see ya' lookin'," she mumbled.

I hadn't been looking at her chest. Quite the opposite, I'd been purposefully maintaining eye contact, and she knew it. The sly grin twitching at the corner of her mouth told me everything I needed to know. She was putting me in my place and enjoying it. This wasn't the first time. She also liked to put me in my place by reminding me I was the youngest of our group. Peter was fourteen, just out of eighth grade like me, but his birthday was in January, a couple of months before mine. Billy, fifteen and coming out of ninth grade, was a little less than a year younger than sixteen-year-old Annie, whose birthday was on St. Patrick's Day, the day after my birthday. Since the time she and I had kissed two years ago, Annie had grown into a different person, still compact, not much taller than when she was fourteen, but with a more commanding presence. She seemed much closer to being a woman than the girl with whom I'd once shared tongues. Still, that kiss lingered in my brain. That kiss.

"Steve! Would ya' quit lookin' at her tits and serve!" Peter yelled. He didn't care if I ogled her; he merely wanted to get in on the fun.

I sighed again, muttered an obligatory, "Screw all y'all," and served. The little white ball fell limply into the net.

"18–20. Game point, your serve, buuuudy." Billy liked to draw out the soft u in buddy.

Behind me, Annie chuckled.

I spun, glaring at her. "See what you did?"

"See what? Did my feet get in the way of your shitty serve? Did I see that you can't serve worth a doggon crap?" She chuckled again and blew a stream of smoke in my direction. I waved it away. "You don't like it? You can go the fuck home." She pointed toward the garage entrance. Then she tucked her legs up in a cross-legged position on the armchair. "There, ya' little wussy. Happy? Let's see you lose this point then. Oh, wait. Here we go!" She leaped up and cranked the knob on the radio sitting on a wooden shelf on the back wall. "There it is! Green grass! Wooh!" She pumped both fists.

Our game stopped.

We shouted the lyrics to "Green Grass and High Tides," the most redneck of all redneck songs. But what could you do, it was a good song. I checked my sneaker laces, which felt loose, and when I looked back up, Billy was inside the garage and dancing with Annie by the refrigerator. His hand rested on the small of her back, their swaying hips fused together. Her left hand lay flat on his right butt cheek, not squeezing it, but just there, sort of casual. This was new. Last year, Annie was with Joey, even though he was my age. Or at least that's where Joey told us he was disappearing all the time. But Joey wasn't around that summer, instead staying at his mom's place in Jamaica

Queens, New York. So, with Joey gone, I suppose it made sense for hot Annie LeFevre and studly Billy Duncan to get together. Billy, with his dark eyebrows, high cheekbones, and sharp brown eyes, was the best looking out of all of us, almost a dead ringer for the actor Sam Elliot, only younger, skinnier, and without the porn-star mustache. As they swung to the rhythm, she squeezed his ass, which I supposed made them an official thing. Did this relationship start that day, or had they been getting together in secret? Was she giving him looks while we were playing ping pong, and, if so, why didn't that help my game any? I shot a confused look at Peter like 'what the heck, dude?' He shrugged like, 'what are ya' gonna do?'

I checked the lovebirds again. Behind them on the back wall, the mustard-colored fridge's door now swung wide, its stark light shining into the dim garage. Annie was reaching into the fridge and handing Billy a beer, a golden bottle of Miller High Life. Where and how did she get a beer? She lived alone with her grandmother in the two-bedroom ranch. Annie never invited us in. We mostly went into her house to use the bathroom. When I did venture inside, the hall from her foyer to the bathroom gave me a direct line of sight to where her grandmother sat in the small sunroom at the back of the house. The woman, her short gray hair cut just above her housecoat's shoulders, was always sitting there, not doing much of anything it seemed, not responding to the sound of the front door opening. Not moving. If I hadn't seen her light a cigarette once, I would have sworn she was dead like Norman Bates's mother in *Psycho*.

Peter popped off his stool. "Hey, you got enough for everyone?"

"Yup. Here, dumbass." She handed him a beer. Her eyes flitted to me for a second, and she handed me one too. "You ever had a full beer, Stevie? Don't get sick in my garage, Baby Huey."

I had never drunk a full beer. I'd shared one with Joey the summer before after he'd sneaked it out of his house. "It's just one beer," I muttered taking a sip and setting it down on a ledge. Annie and Billy, back to dancing, fronts pressed together, her tank top smushed against his bare chest, began kissing open mouthed.

So, that's what it looked like when she French kissed me.

Peter had returned to perch on his stool. "Get a room."

Billy responded by laughing, and Annie grabbed Billy's hand, opened the back door to the garage, and wordlessly led him into the house. The door clicked shut behind them.

"Wow," Peter breathed. "I didn't mean it."

"See what you made them do!" I exclaimed with a note of amusement.

Peter smiled and took a deep drink from the bottle, the yellow liquid disappearing with a glug-glug as he tilted it back.

"What do you think they're going to do?" I asked, knowing the answer.

Peter shot me a look like 'what do you think?'

"With her grandmother in the house?"

"Dude, you know her grandmother's not all there, right? She's like smoking weed back there in the porch sometimes. Annie rolls joints and gives them to her to keep her from wandering outside. That's why Annie isn't in school anymore since January. The lady's got...I forget the word."

"Senility?"

"Something. She stares at nothing back there, man. It's old-timer's disease."

"Hmm." That word didn't sound exactly right, but I didn't know the correct term, so I let it go.

Peter drained his bottle. "We should steal her grandmother's pot. This is the perfect time while they're doing it. I know where it is. It's in this little brown jewelry box in the old lady's room."

So many questions raced through my head: How did Peter know all this? Was Annie's grandmother actually brain-dead? How long would Annie and Billy—presumably in Annie's bedroom—take to finish doing it? Could I really steal marijuana from a poor old lady? There were only two bedrooms in the house as far as I knew, and they were across the hall from each other, so would Annie and Billy hear us entering and rifling through stuff in the other room?

Peter was already halfway through the garage door and into the house, beckoning me with a sharp wave. "Come on, bitch."

Don't go in there. Stay out here, Shpresa admonished me.

My little-big friend had been relatively quiet over the last week or two since school let out, so when she hissed into my ear, I physically lurched and stepped back.

Peter screwed up his face at me. "You that afraid? I'm going in. Come on."

Don't go in there.

Don't tell me what to do, Shpresa. You're dead.

I sprang forward and caught the front doorknob an instant before the door slipped closed. Peter halted in the foyer, waiting for me as I slid inside the house. Out back in the sunroom, as promised, Annie's grandmother, her profile to us, sat quietly, smoking a joint, not a cigarette as I'd thought. She mechanically lifted it to her lips, puffing, and dropping it back to her lap each time she exhaled. I couldn't see where the joint went when she lowered it, so I wondered if she was in danger of burning herself. I didn't have time to get an answer because Peter was on the move, and I followed him. We turned right and tiptoed through the hallway toward the bedrooms.

16

There's still time to go. Turn around. Walk out.

Quiet, Shpresa.

As we approached the bedrooms, her grandmother's door open, Annie's closed, my ears perked to a soft *thump–thump–thump* repeating from behind the closed bedroom door. Peter walked a couple of feet in front of me, and, after stopping at Annie's door to listen to the thumping, he pointed at the open door across the hall and touched an index finger to his lips.

Neither of us entered her grandmother's room right away, though. We stood still for a few moments, listening to the *thump–thump–thump*. The knocking continued, followed by high-pitched moans that had to be Annie and a groan that must have been Billy. Peter smirked and grabbed his crotch, and I rolled my eyes at him. The noises and knocking trailed off into silence. I gazed at the wooden door and wondered exactly what had just happened. All the details.

They're done, Steven. That was them finishing. They did it the regular way. Missionary. And you know he's got a big one if you feel like picturing it.

I wasn't sure I felt like picturing it. How did Shpresa know that fact about Billy? Last summer, we'd camped out in a tent in the middle of the field across the street from Annie's house. Annie hadn't been there, just four of us guys—Joey, Billy, Peter, and me. Rob, as usual, was holed up inside his house, maybe reading. We'd taken turns showing each other our flaccid penises by the light of a kerosene lantern—in hindsight a dangerous thing, a lantern like that in a tent…or, might I add, its flame near our penises. My penis, I thought, was average, about the same size as Peter's. Joey's, even though he was the shortest of us, was larger than average. Then Billy whipped his out. His was the biggest by far, and there was an awkward silence, followed by Peter shouting, "Yo, that's a big dick!" making us all laugh.

Staring at Billy's oversized member had made me feel...

Jealous. You're jealous of your friend's big penis. It's okay. When I was alive, I was jealous of girls with bigger boobs than me. Admit it and move on.

Screw you, Shpresa...You're right.

For the first time, I wondered if this voice tickling the inside rim of my ear might simply be *me* speaking to myself, even though the hairs inside my ear canal seemed to rustle as her words entered my mind, almost as if Shpresa was blowing a warm, faint breeze into my head.

One last chance not to follow Peter in that room.

Screw you. Don't tell me what to do. I tell me what to do.

I followed Peter into the open bedroom. The sharp sting of moth balls, mixed with the underlying musty odor of old newspapers, assaulted my nostrils. There were stacks and stacks of newspapers in the bedroom, foot-high cubes tied together with twine and piled several feet high upon each other. These teetering newspaper towers, a Seussian nightmare, formed a maze around the thin slices of visible threadbare carpet, multiple paths that all led toward an unmade Queen bed on the far wall. Beside the bed, Peter stood in front of a nicked-up, low wooden dresser with a mirror on its top. He opened a small wooden box on the dresser and produced a baggie near bursting with what had to be pot. I approached him, and he grabbed the outside lip of my front shorts pocket, startling me. He tipped the baggie, shaking it so about half of its brown grass spilled into my pocket.

"What the hell are you doing?" I whispered.

He rolled up the baggie and placed it back in the box, after which he leaned toward me and spoke into my ear, his breath smelling faintly of beer. "My shorts don't have pockets, so you gotta hold it. We can't take it all." He was right, he wore black St. Theresa's Middle School athletic shorts without pockets, only a bright red line up each side.

He hustled to the doorway and waved me out hurriedly. I raised my eyes and caught my reflection in the mirror. One word flashed into my head: *Thief*.

I'm not sure if it was Shpresa talking to me or me talking to myself.

Peter was skittering down the short hall and around the corner as I stepped into the hallway. I hesitated in front of Annie's bedroom door. It was quiet. I jumped backward as the door swung open and Annie appeared in front of me, dressed only in light pink underpants and clutching her balled-up yellow tank top to her chest. Behind her, visible through the partly open door, Billy leaned his head against her headboard, his abdominal muscles taut and a sheet draped over his lower body. "Stevieeee!" he exclaimed laughingly, chin-nodding as if to say 'look at me, it's cool, baby' like Danny Zuko from *Grease*.

Despite myself, I nodded back at him before returning my focus to Annie. She glared at me. "I thought I heard something out here. What are you doing, Stevie?" She didn't bother to lower her voice.

I froze, not sure what to say as my cheeks grew warm. It looked like I was creeping around listening to them screw. And she was partially right, we had been listening to them although that hadn't been our main goal. I couldn't tell her we stole some of her grandma's pot, could I? She had no clue.

I thought about walking into her grandmother's room and putting the pot back as well as I could, and—

No. Just walk away. She thinks you're a perv. Leave it at that.

Good idea, Shpresa.

Finally. Now you're listening to me.

I smiled thinly at Annie, saying nothing, and marched down the short hall. As I was about to turn the corner, she yelled at my back, "Perv! Get your own girl." I stopped. "Here, you wanna see my tits,

Stevie?" Her yellow shirt hit the back of my head and dropped behind me on the hallway floor. "You can check 'em out. Like 'em jerkwad?"

Don't turn. It's not what she really wants.

Don't turn? She's inviting me. Despite my better instincts and Shpresa's caution, I rotated. Annie's chest, flushed and with a sheen of perspiration glittering under her neck, rose and fell, and her flat, tanned stomach moved in and out in time with her chest as if she was angry or out of breath or both. I stepped toward her, stopping halfway up the hall.

I looked at her. I purposefully, intently looked. After all, she'd given me permission.

"There you go. Like them tits, asshole?"

I did. "They're fine." I bent, picked up her shirt, and tossed it to her. I swallowed hard and headed around the corner. "Sorry," I replied over my shoulder as I opened the inside garage door.

I was sorry, but not mostly for the thing she thought I was sorry about.

Hiding the Stash

My cousin Cher came to live with us last summer when I was thirteen. My mom liked to say that Cher's dad, my mom's brother Damon, was, in her humble opinion, a 'bonafide no-good.' Cher, whose full name was Cheryl Rankin, but who adored the famous singer, Cher, told me her dad drank too much. But one time she mentioned something about pills, too, so maybe I didn't know the whole story about my Uncle Damon. Cher's mom had disappeared into the wind long ago.

Our ranch house, on a manmade lake in the heart of Oakland Park, wasn't that large as far as square feet, but it possessed four compact bedrooms. The smallest bedroom was the size of a large walk-in closet — barely big enough for a twin bed and a dresser. That's the room I took when Cher moved in. I liked Cher, so I was fine with her taking the third-smallest bedroom even though she asked me repeatedly if I wanted her to take the smallest bedroom.

Most days, my parents fussed about money. Their voices whistled across the house like two kitchen knives clinking against each other, and their conversations would rip to a stop if one of us kids entered the room. But even though money was tight, my mom declared, with a little fist-pound-into-palm thing and a slight tilt of her head, that a *good Christian* would always take in someone in need. I never reminded her that Cher was family, so, in my mind, we had to take her in anyway. Reminding my mom of anything, even that we were late for church, never went well. It wasn't my place.

There was about a two-year gap between each of us three kids living in the house: nearly eighteen-year-old Cher, my sixteen-year-old sister, Marie, and fourteen-year-old me. But from the look of it, you'd never know Cher had graduated high school that June and that Marie was only going into the eleventh grade. Cher wore plain, long, periwinkle and light-yellow floral-print dresses. Marie wore tight Jordache jeans, shiny satin 'disco' blouses in purple and cream tones, and faux-leather knee boots or high heels, the latter of which my mom was constantly trying to confiscate from her room. Cher, mousy brown hair waterfalling straight to the middle of her back, rarely wore makeup; Marie, especially on Saturday nights, wore pink eyeshadow and bright ruby lipstick, and my sister curled her blonde tresses to fall in waves like the hairstyle of Farrah Fawcett, one of *Charlie's Angels*.

My cousin Cher stayed in most nights, except this past spring when she ventured out a bunch of times with her friend from Oakland Park High, Dona, who would pick her up to go to Movie City 11. When Cher wasn't going out, she almost always seemed to be studying for a prep course she was taking in advance of community college in the fall. Like a lot of families, our parents didn't have the money to send her to a four-year college, even to a state school like Florida State.

During that summer of 1980, and come to think of it, during the school year before that, my sister went out more evenings than not with some of the older kids in the neighborhood. Marie missed her curfew at least a couple of times, but she never got in trouble. Sometimes my mother's bark would wake me up past midnight, and I knew she'd caught Marie sneaking in. But as far as I could tell there weren't any consequences beyond the shouting. In her vanity drawer, my sister kept a fake ID, which she'd gotten in Coconut Grove down in Miami. I stole a little of her marijuana once and smoked it with Peter down in the field by Annie's. I was glad my sister never caught me stealing that marijuana from her. I was sure it would be me who somehow got in big trouble, not Marie. My parents talked about pot as 'evil' and 'the flower of Satan,' so I would have been harshly punished, and Marie somehow would have wriggled out of it. She was like that—she had good hiding places, and she was slick like a non-stick pan, trouble sliding off her easy as a buttery fried egg off Teflon.

But sometimes, Marie's aura of invincibility could be useful. That's why, after I bicycled back from Annie's that Saturday, barely beating an afternoon storm, I rushed into my older sister's room and closed her door. I pressed the lock. "Hey, Marie."

"Uh, *hello?*" Marie, perched at her vanity and brushing her golden hair, had this way of addressing me like every little thing I did was some gigantic offense to her.

"Hello." I ignored her tone, pretending her response was a pleasant greeting rather than a show of attitude. "I need you to do me a favor...please."

She continued brushing her hair. The song "Summer Nights" from *Grease* played for the one-hundred thousandth frigging time on her record player. "Is that so? You need a favor? That's why you locked my door?"

That's what he said, Marie, you bitch.

Why did Shpresa pick now to chime in? And she seemed especially angry at Marie. Why? Did I feel the same way?

Shh. Be nice, Shpresa.

"Yeah, I need a favor, please. If you do me a favor, I'll owe you."

My sister folded her arms across her low-cut, lavender satin blouse. She was dressed up because it was Saturday night, and she was going out. "We're not going to a teen disco. I can't take you out tonight if that's what you want, Steven."

"No, not that."

Although that would have been fun.

I dipped my hand into my high-cut shorts. How was I going to get the pot out of my pants even? I knew Marie had baggies in her vanity drawer. I wiggled my fingers through the vegetation inside my pocket, my fingertips stumbling over seeds and stems. "I–I need a baggie."

"A baggie?" A dubious look crossed her face.

I sighed, walked to her vanity, and shook out the contents of my pocket onto a clear space on its top. The resulting mound on her beige vanity was about ninety-seven percent marijuana, including stems and seeds, with about three percent pocket lint mixed in. She laughed, picking a piece of lint from the top of the mound. "Look at you, Steven. Where did you—"

"Can't say. Can I have a baggie?"

"Ooookay." She bagged the pile for me, using a small, wide-mouthed funnel and a ruler to push the grass from the vanity and into a small, clear plastic bag. She twist-tied it and handed it back. "Favor done. Have fun. Looks skunky though."

"Also, uh, can you hide it for me please?" That was the real favor.

"What?"

"In your—" She didn't know that I knew where she hid her pot.

"In. My. *What?*" Her mouth had gone small, and her crystal blue eyes bit into my flesh. Whoops.

"In your boot." I swallowed hard.

She squinted at me. "Hmm. My boot, huh? You can hide it yourself in your own room, you little sneak. And stay out of here."

"My room's so small. There's nowhere good." That was the truth. And my mom still cleaned my room, even though I told her I could clean it myself. "Mom's in there sometimes. She'd find it."

Marie's bedroom was in the front of our house, with two large windows facing the street. As I finished my sentence, the storm that had chased me from Annie's grumbled like an angry giant. The sky darkened outside and burst open, fat drops pattering on the hibiscus bushes in front of Marie's windows. Neither of us paid the rain any mind. In South Florida, we were used to the occasional heavy afternoon shower, which boiled up over the Everglades, raced toward shore like a gray sweeping curtain hanging from towering black clouds, and caught our home in its thundering wake.

She eyed the pile of marijuana. "Looks like a little more than an eighth. I'll roll a joint for myself, and I'll hide the rest for you. But you can't come take it back yourself. You need to ask me for it. No snooping in my stuff, or I'll make sure you get busted. Get it, sprout?"

Sprout. I understood her threat.

Wow. Your sister is truly awful, threatening you with that. Also, I thought she said it was skunky? Why would she want to smoke any of it?

Shhh, Shpresa! I'm bargaining here.

"Deal, Marie."

"No, it's not a deal. I don't deal with you," my sister answered with a huff.

Well, it was a deal, but I didn't push the point. I handed the baggie to her as our front door erupted with a pounding. Somebody outside was beating up its wooden panels.

"Who the hell is out front?" my sister muttered, lifting the needle on her phonograph to restart her favorite song. She slid open her closet door, reached down, and buried the baggie deep inside her weed boot. Then she opened her bedroom door and shooed me out. "Go. Get."

My mom, her beehive, blonde hairdo high upon her head, swished down the hall toward my sister's room. The chain around my mother's neck centered a small golden cross firmly over her high-collared burnt-orange blouse. "Steven, your little friend is at the door."

"Uh, for me? Friend?" Could she mean Peter? He was about five-seven, an inch shorter than me, but that's not really little.

My mom grabbed a freshly folded bath towel from our hall closet. "Yes, your little *friend*." She spun and walked around the corner, and I followed her toward our front door.

Annie, all five feet and three inches of her, arms folded across her chest, wet hair scraggly, dripped on the linoleum tile of the open hallway into our house. The girl's eyes burned into me. I'd known Annie for maybe four or five years, and she'd never visited my house.

She's here for her pot, dummy. Told you not to go into that bedroom.

No duh, Shpresa. Shh.

I told you.

Shut it.

My mom handed Annie the towel. The girl dried her wet stringy hair, patted her body, and handed the damp towel back to my mother. "Thank you, Mrs. Jacobs."

"You're very welcome, dear." My mom showed no intention of leaving us.

"Annie. Uh, what's up?"

"Hey, Stevie. The rain just stopped. Let's go outside." Annie turned to my mom. "It was nice to meet you Mrs. Jacobs. Thank you, again, for the towel. Storm came in fast and got me."

"You're more than welcome. It was nice to meet you as well, Anne."

"It's Analynn. One word."

I did not know Annie's full name was Analynn.

"Analynn."

Cher was studying at the table in the dining room on the other side of the waist-high wall that ran down the front hallway. She'd been quiet through this entire encounter, but as my mother said 'Analynn,' my cousin stuck up her head, her large, translucent-pink-framed glasses nosing up to check us out.

Annie nodded toward my front door, and I opened it for her.

"Be home by six for dinner," my mom said to me as my sister Marie, without acknowledging our existence, weaved past Annie and me in the foyer hall and flew out the open front door. Marie hurried to the black El Camino that had pulled out of Joey's driveway down the street and backed up to idle at our curb. I assumed my mom was talking to me about getting home for dinner on time because my sister was obviously going out for the night, picked up by Joey's brother, Sal, a rising senior at Oakland Park High and her on-and-off boyfriend. The El Camino growled and rumbled down the road, and my mom watched it leave with defeat in her blue eyes. Then my mother shooed us outside and shut the front door, leaving me on the front stoop with Annie's rage-contorted face—her lips pressed together, jaw clenching and unclenching, and light brown eyes blazing at me like the fires of hell.

"Give me my grandmother's stash. You stole half of it," she hissed.

"What? Stash?"

Good, you're playing dumb. You're good at that.

Why now, Shpresa?

"Don't 'what' me, Stevie. You were standing right outside her bedroom door, and when I went to roll my grandma a joint, somebody done stole half her grass. Did you really steal from an old lady? I buy it with her Social Security checks. You know, I bust your balls, but I thought we was friends."

I did steal it. We stole it. And my face must have shown how guilty I felt because her eyes widened, and she claimed, "You did steal it, you jerk. I can see it in your eyes. You go inside right now and get my grandma's shit!" She was yelling now.

"I can't."

"You better, or I'm gonna ask your mom for it."

She's not going to do that.

I considered running into the house and grabbing the baggie. Then I recalled my sister telling me she'd get me in trouble, suggesting she'd make my parents send me away if she discovered I ventured into her room again.

I gulped. "You're not going to tell my mom. My, uh, sister took it. To hide it for me outside of the house."

Her slender pointer finger found its way to the center of my bony chest. "That's bullcrap. It's in your house. I'll get somebody to kick your ass. Don't think I won't. Not Billy or them either, somebody who don't know you. Not like a black eye. He'll break your ribs and knock out your teeth. My second cousin's in the Hells Angels. He knows plenty of guys." She closed her mouth tight, her fingertip a sharp stick against my chest.

Beads of sweat broke out on my forehead. She was serious. "Okay. I'll grab it."

The words were barely out of my mouth when the flat of her palm stung my cheek. I grabbed my tingling jaw and stepped back in shock. Her face had gone red and scrunchy, and a tear squeezed from her eye. "Annie, I..."

"You jerkwad, you did take it, and then you're gonna lie about where it is?" she breathed. "Taking advantage of me. Go get me my grandma's pot."

28

With my hand plastered to my stinging cheek, I walked, numb, like a zombie from that movie, *Dawn of the Dead*, to my sister's room. I didn't even bother to close Marie's door. I opened her closet slider, bent down, and stuck my hand inside her boot. My fingertips hit the insole. I reached farther in. Nothing. The weed boot was empty.

"No, no, no," I breathed, extracting my hand, a chill racing down my spine and a thick knot forming in my throat.

Marie hid it from you.

"What are you doing in here?" My mom stood in the doorway.

My mind raced to think of something. "Uh..."

"Your friend is very cute, but you can't borrow your sister's shoes for the girl. What are you thinking? Out of here, Steven." My mom pointed down the hall.

At least she created an alibi for why you were in here.

"Out! She's outside, and she's crying." My mom's eyes narrowed. She must have been spying on Annie through the front window. "What did you do to that little girl?"

Ooh, she thinks you screwed Annie LeFevre or something.

"She's a friend. Somebody did her wrong. She's just a friend."

"Mmm, hmm. Steven, how old is this girl?"

"Uh, sixteen, I think. Just turned."

My mom became perfectly still for a long, painful moment, except for an almost imperceptible twitch in one eye. "She's going into eleventh grade?"

Annie wasn't going into any grade as far as I knew unless the authorities caught up with her. But my mom's point was clear: Annie was two years older than me.

"She's sort of going out with Billy who's going into tenth." I don't know why I thought this would make things better in my mom's head.

"Go out there, and send that girl home, and then I want you inside."

29

I obeyed her. My shoulders sagged as I trudged down the hall, the pit in my stomach growing as large and heavy as the black holes we learned about in gifted class. Like no light could escape the inky tendrils of fear spreading through my midsection.

Annie was wiping her eyes when I rejoined her on the porch. "You got it?"

"I swear, I gave the stuff to my sister to keep for me, but she hid it on me. And now she's out with Sal and them, and my mom caught me in there. I'll get it tomorrow. I swear. I'm sorry." I said all this in a flurry.

She shook her head in disgust. "You better get it back! You got two days 'til Monday. Or I swear, I'm gonna get someone to beat you with a lead pipe. Does Peter have any of it?"

How could she know it was Peter? She's fishing.

"No."

She spun and stormed down my walkway. She was wearing shoes, unusual for her. They were slip-on boat shoes that looked about twenty years old, with a graying rubber lining enclosing the worn, soft blue cloth of the actual shoe.

"Annie, can I still come over tomorrow if the others do?"

She stopped and twisted her head but not her body to study me. "If Billy and them come over, you do what you like. But if you gotta piss, go outside in the field. You stay out of my house. And if you don't gimme my grandma's weed by tomorrow or Monday, don't ever bother coming back. I thought we was friends, Stevie. Friends don't pull that crud. Look at the nice house you got up here. Like I got all the money in the world to buy grass."

My house wasn't anything special, but I never considered that it was bigger and nicer than her grandmother's two-bedroom ranch. "I'm sorry. I really am, Annie."

I told you.

I sighed. *You did, Shpresa. Okay?*

Annie was square with me now, several yards away, like a gunfight was about to go down. "You 'member when I kissed you?"

"Yes." I'd never forget it. I'd never forget the electricity that ran through my body. The sparks and the colors in my mind. The feel of her soft wet tongue swirling around mine.

"You know why I did it?"

"No." I never asked her why. Never asked for more than I got that day.

"Joey put me up to kissing you. They all did. Him, Billy, and Peter. And I figured you wouldn't mind."

"Oh." Now that she'd said it, I had to admit that I suspected that was the reason.

"They wanted to see how bad you were at it. Wanted to see you choke on yer own spit." She paused. "But you was okay. It backfired on 'em. It was a good long kiss, right? Joey got all jealous about it later."

I could think of nothing to say in response to this.

"Stevie, you know Billy and them think you're a joke, right? They don't think you're any better than that book-sissy, Rob Sheldon down the road. You should hear 'em talk about you and him when you're not around. So, yeah, you can come by my house for the next couple days. But even if you give back my grandma's pot, you and me ain't gonna be good friends no more. And now you got no real friends because they all just wanna make fun of you. I might have busted your balls, but at least I liked you. *Used* to like you. So, give back my grass, or it's gonna be trouble." She wiped at her eye one last time. And she was off.

Darn.

Darn indeed.

Quiet, Shpresa. Please.

I tried to stay awake until my sister came home. I fell asleep on the family room couch sometime after midnight, watching a movie playing on *Big Wilson's Night Owl Theater*. I woke at about one thirty in the morning to the not-so-faint sounds of Marie and my mother arguing on the other side of the house, a door slamming. I dragged my dark blue Star Wars comforter down the hall toward my bedroom. My parents' door was closed. Marie's door, facing me from the other end of the hall, was closed. Cher's door, several feet down from Marie's, was closed, too.

I tap–tap–tapped on Marie's door. Nothing. Tapped again, lightly. "Go away," came Marie's muffled voice through the wood.

I pressed my forehead against her door. "Marie," I whispered. "Marie."

"Go away."

Down the hall, my parents' bedroom door swung open. My mother, in a white cotton nightgown, poked her head out, her usually coiffed blonde hair wild, dark rings under her eyes. "Steven!" Her low voice whipped at me. "Leave your sister alone." My mom's head vanished into her room.

Get it tomorrow. Go to sleep.

Don't tell me what to do, Shpresa.

But I listened to Shpresa anyway. I went to bed, tossed and turned for a while, and woke up too late, after the damage had already been done.

32

Patsy

Sunday

I woke up too late. My alarm clock read two in the afternoon. That couldn't be right. My mom had let me skip Sunday church?

I picked crusty granules of sleep from my eyes as I sat on the edge of my bed in my saggy white underwear. Why did I feel like somebody hit me on the head?

Guilt is weighing on you.

I ignored Shpresa. I slipped on some shorts and a tank top, and I ambled down the hall toward the kitchen in search of Lucky Charms.

Before I got to the kitchen, I walked by a strange scene. My family sat in the open sunken living room at the back of our house, across from the foyer hallway and tiny dining room by the front door. All four of them: my dad and my mom on the sofa, Marie and Cher on the loveseat at a right angle. My dad, a gangly praying mantis in olive church slacks and a loosened green tie over a cream shirt, sat hunched with his arms folded and his jaw clenched. His balding, graying light-brown hair was cut close, and his gold-rimmed spectacles hung menacingly near the end of his nose. My mom was still in a church dress, dark green to match my dad's outfit, her blonde hair and cross as perfect as perfect could be. My sister, her golden hair still curled from the night before, wore shorts and a T-shirt, no shoes. Marie was certainly not wearing church clothes; last year, my mom gave up trying to make her attend church. Marie sat closer to my parents, and her face was turned toward the back window behind them, away from Cher, who sat on the far side of the love seat. Cher also wore shorts and a T-shirt, and her reddened face was streaked with tears. When she saw me, she hid her face in her hands, and her shoulders shuddered as she started to sob.

Jesus. What the heck is going on?

This is the aftermath, Steven.

I stood at the lip of the single step that descended into the shallow living room. "What's going on? Cher, why are you crying?"

Marie, a hard look on her face, stood and bolted past me, grumbling, "That's what you two get for not trusting me. Maybe next time you'll listen and believe me." She stomped down the hallway toward her room.

Marie's acting insulted, Steven. Acting.

I know she's acting. Or, yeah, I thought so.

"Steven, sit." My mom pointed to the empty space by Cher. I sat on the love seat, filling the warm depression left by Marie. On the other side of the small sofa, Cher turned away from me. No longer sobbing, hand over her face.

My dad held up two baggies filled with marijuana. One was the baggie of Annie's pot. The other baggie was larger, and the grass it held was darker and dotted by a handful of small, round, white pills. "Do you know about this, Steven?"

Darn! I shook my head but didn't answer, afraid the lump and tremor burbling up inside my throat would make my voice crack and give me away. "Mmm, mmm."

"You sure?"

Cher sniffed and wiped her eyes and face with the backs of her wrists. "I told you, it's mine. Everything you found was mine. The pot. The pills. All of it."

Wait, why was Cher saying this was hers? It wasn't hers.

"Steven, go to your room or go outside. We need to speak with Cher." My mother pointed down the hall.

I obeyed. In my room, I thought about heading outside or to Marie's room. But I stayed there and flipped through an Encyclopedia, Volume C. I learned a caribou was the same as a reindeer—pretty much useless information in this situation.

My sister's footsteps tromped down the hall about a half hour later. The front door opened and closed. She'd left the house. A few minutes after that, Cher's bedroom door—halfway between Marie's and mine— opened with a creak and closed with a soft click. I opened my bedroom door and craned my head out. My parents' murmurs echoed in the living room. I tiptoed to Cher's door and knocked lightly.

"Come in."

I eased open her door. She sat on her bed, reading a paperback book. *To Kill a Mockingbird.*

"Hey." She sniffed. Her eyelids were heavy, rimmed red. She leaned over and patted her comforter near her feet. "Close my door. Sit, kiddo." I did both, sitting beside her bare feet and dangling my legs off the edge of her bed.

"What—what happened, Cher?"

She sighed. "We went to church earlier. Aunt Linnea tried to wake you up, but you wouldn't budge. You were out cold."

35

"Okay. But what happened?"

"After church, your mom was making lunch, and your dad took a nap in Marie's room. Your sister had gone outside with Sal or something. I don't know."

"So?" My dad sometimes took weekend afternoon naps in my sister's room when she was out because Marie had the nicest mattress in the house. I'd caught him sleeping in there before in the daytime. Also, it was as far away as you could get from the family room, where my mom watched church programs on Sunday afternoons.

"He found a jar under her mattress. Like *The Princess and the Pea*." She chuckled in a way that suggested she found nothing funny about what she'd said. "A jar with two pot baggies and some pills. He confronted Marie, and she denied it was hers."

A nervous laugh escaped my lips. "But it was her room where he found it. Not yours."

Cher sighed again, a heavy sigh like a weight rested on her chest. "She said it was mine. There was some yelling. I'm surprised you didn't wake up. You were asleep like the dead. Marie said she needed to talk to me alone, and she grabbed me, and we talked out back by the lake."

"Oookay."

Cher wiped at her eye, then her other eye as tears slipped out, plunking onto her bare knees. "She was right. I–I had to admit it was mine, Steven." She rubbed at her face again, blinking back more tears. "Marie was holding it for me. I couldn't let her…"

Bullcrap, Steven. It's bullcrap.

"That's bullcrap." I echoed Shpresa's sentiment.

Cher's head jerked back. "No. It's true."

I lowered my voice. "I know it's not true. I trust you, Cher. You've always been nice to me."

So unlike Marie.

36

"Same." Cher's hand warmed my shoulder.

I kept my voice low. "I know it wasn't yours because one of those bags was mine. I was holding it for a friend. I know the pot wasn't yours. So, why are you covering for her? Don't."

"I'm no narc," she mumbled, inspecting her toenails, painted white.

"There's a difference between being a narc and taking a fall." I thought of the word conspiracy theorists used to describe Lee Harvey Oswald because they didn't believe he killed JFK by himself: patsy. "Why would you be her patsy?"

Cher shook her head. "I can't tell you. I wish I could. It's already...too much has happened."

I stood. "I'm going to tell them the small baggie was mine and that the rest is Marie's."

I blinked, and like a sentry, Cher barred my way to her door. Her hand latched onto my arm with a steely grip, tugging me back toward her bed. "Don't do that Steven. You can't."

"But I've got—"

"They're sending me to The Sprout. You know what that is? Don't get yourself in trouble like that. You need to keep quiet." Her eyes grew wide, pleading.

I gulped and closed my eyes, my stomach reeling. This was out of control. Of course, I knew what The Sprout was. It was a drug rehabilitation center founded by a preacher named Howel Carnavale in 1971. It was in the local news three years back when it won a lawsuit brought by a couple who claimed people in charge of the program brainwashed and cruelly harassed their teenage son, who then took his own life. The specter of this place, out in nowheresville Everglades — where the ocean boiled its water, where the staff kept you up all night and yelled at you until you broke — was murmured and mumbled about by parents and kids alike. It was a horror story told at camp to keep teens in line, akin to something out of the film, *Friday the Thirteenth*, which had just come out. Women from my mom's church circle uttered the name, 'The Sprout' to their teens the same way they would say 'Hell' to scare their small children, hanging it over their heads as a potential consequence of drug use, any waywardness really. Often, kids who went into The Sprout were forced to pick between juvenile detention and time in the rehab. Some kids, so afraid of the rehab, chose juvie. Julie Johnson, the daughter of my mom's good friend, Cynthia Johnson, had been sent to the Sprout last summer, and Cynthia swore by it. I'd overheard the woman at our church one morning claiming The Sprout, praise Jesus, had returned her daughter to her. Meanwhile, Julie, a silent puppet in a long dress, her eyes as vacant as those of a Stepford wife, stood beside her mother. Rebuilt. Clean. Emptied and refilled.

"You can't go, Cher. They can't send you there. You're out of high school."

"I'm not eighteen until early September. And they've already called the police. I've got no choice."

"No! No." I was up and pacing.

"It'll be fine. It's two months, then a month living in somebody else's home if I play it right. I'll be out in time to reenroll at BCC."

"But you don't even smoke."

She stared at her toes some more. "I tried it once. With Sal."

"Sal? Sal Bucci?" My sister's…whatever. "When did you hang with Sal Bucci?"

She gulped, and her eyes widened as if she'd said too much. "You need to keep quiet, kiddo. Keep your head down." Her eyes flitted to her window, where the branches of a small palm occluded the view of the house next door. "I can trust you. Right? You keep secrets."

"Yes." I did keep secrets.

She was so, so quiet. Then she spoke. "I was seeing Sal. He broke up with Marie for like five months almost. He and I met at school in gym. We were sneaking around. Down the beach. All over the place for three months this spring. Your sister didn't know at first. He's so sweet. I–I really liked him."

Sure, Sal is sweet and nice, with a welcoming smile. Sal is movie-star hot, even better looking than his brother Joey. Better looking than Shaun Cassidy. Everybody knows Sal, Shpresa opined.

Cher isn't bad looking either, I guess. I never thought about her that way before, though, as somebody's girlfriend. She hid herself, literally and figuratively. Still, wow. Sal Bucci.

So much you didn't know was happening right under your nose, Steve.

"Shut up, Shpresa."

"What?" Cher, her brows knitted together, looked hurt.

"Sorry, I was thinking out loud. So, why? What does Sal have to do with anything? I don't understand."

"Promise to keep quiet? Forever?"

"Swear. Forever."

She sighed. "I got pregnant. You know about all that, right?"

I nodded, trying to keep the shock off my face from this revelation, but probably not doing a good job. Also, I'd known how babies were made since early in sixth grade when a bunch of us boys at lunch tried our best to convince pimply Dickie Straw, who led a sheltered life, that there was no Santa Claus. The subject had turned to sex, which really blew Dickie's mind.

Cher continued. "Marie found out I was pregnant and that it was Sal's. At first, she was stinking mad. Then she took me to get an abortion. That was early May. It was the weekend I was supposed to be staying at Dona's, and Marie was supposed to be at her friend Helen's."

"Oh." I couldn't think of anything else to say. I remembered that weekend. Did Cher or Marie act funny at the time? I couldn't recall.

Tears again flowed down Cher's cheeks, and it was all I could do not to wipe them off.

"Marie told me to say the drugs were mine, or she'd tell your mom about the abortion. I can't let your mom know I got an abortion. She would kick me out if she knew. You know how Aunt Linnea is. I don't have anywhere else to go. So, this isn't so bad."

"Maybe she wouldn't kick you out." I didn't believe it either. I knew she would kick her out. I'd heard my mom go completely off the rails crazy about how abortion is pure evil. And I wasn't sure she ever wanted Cher to stay with us in the first place.

"It's not so bad going to The Sprout. I'll be okay."

Marie gets off scot-free.

"I'm sorry." I reached over, and I instinctively wrapped my cousin in a hug. "I'm so sorry, Cher."

She patted my back like I was the one who needed comforting. "I'll never tell on you, Steven. I promise. You're a good kid." She sniffed. "It's three months. I'll be fine."

'I'll be fine.' I wondered why she kept saying that. 'I'll be fine.'

Promises were made that day.

Lies were told.

An innocent person was convicted and sentenced, and it was all my fault.

But I figured Cher would come back, and it would get better.

Cher came back in November of that year.

Well, somebody came back to us.

"The Sprout, No Doubt"

[Sung to the melody of "What Child Is This?" or "Greensleeves"]

The Sprout, no doubt
Is all about
Washing the weed and the pills right out
Get up each day from dawn past dusk
The branch of the Sprout
Is what we trust
And if we fail
We will not shout
We'll scrub ourselves harder
To get the stain out

Honor, Sorrow, and Revenge

Monday

I sat on the kitchen counter as far as the uncoiled cord allowed, staring at the mustard yellow receiver hanging on the brown-and-white striped wallpaper. I waited for my friend to answer. He did, picking up after three rings. "Stevie. *My* man."

His man, yeah, right. I was his man. More like his fall guy. "Petey."

"Where were you yesterday, Stevie? Boy, you're in trouble with Annie."

I lowered my voice. "I need you to tell her that I need one more day. I'll come down to her house tomorrow. Things are bad here, dude. It's crazy. My parents took off work today. Right now, they went out to breakfast, then to pick up legal papers from somewhere, but they called from a payphone and said they'll be home soon. Marie's asleep in her room. Dude, my dad found a bunch of drugs and gave it to the police. He found Annie's stuff, too, so it's gone. Tomorrow, they're taking Cher to The Sprout."

Peter sucked in a sharp breath when I mentioned The Sprout. "Damn. Cher?"

"Yeah." I hoped he wouldn't ask me questions as to why Cher was going to rehab.

It's all your fault, Steven. And Peter's. You both stole the pot. You gave it to your sister. And it wasn't the first time you stole pot. You stole a joint's worth from Marie earlier in the year to impress Carrie Sullivan at school. That's how you knew where Marie hid her stash. That's why she moved her stash. That's why your father found it. It's all your fault.

You're right, Shpresa, it was my fault.

"Cher, huh?" Peter repeated her name. "Man, your cousin got corrupted. She went out with Salvatore for three months, and now she's headed to rehab. And some of that pot was ours, too. That stinks."

Our pot. Ugh. Wait, he knew Cher was with Sal? "How did you know Cher was with Sal?"

"Joey told me. He thought it was crazy, but I get it. Your cousin's got some big tits. She's pretty hot, yo. I'd do her."

To be honest, I never noticed Cher like that. Also, it made me grit my teeth, his talking about her like she was nothing more than a couple of walking boobs. "Stop, man. Don't talk about Cher like that."

"Whatever."

"Just tell Annie I'll get her the stuff tomorrow."

There was silence on the line.

"Petey? You there?"

"You're stand-up, Stevie. Annie told us she went to your house. You kept your mouth shut and didn't narc me out. You did the right thing."

"Yeah." I sighed.

Boys. Always with your messed-up ideas about loyalty and honor.
Whatever.

43

"One day is all I need, Petey. Marie and I will be alone tomorrow. She'll go out. She always does. Then I'll get what Annie needs." I was hoping beyond hope Marie had replenished her stash.

"Okay. We're going down there to play ping pong today. Billy and Annie do it every day now. She's got a friend, Sharon, who might come over. Supposed to be hot. You're gonna miss out."

I laughed. "You mean they did it yesterday and the day before."

"Dude, they were screwing way before that. Like since school let out. Using condoms and everything. And she's taking the pill, so she doesn't get pregnant."

"Oh."

"Yeah."

"I'll come by Annie's tomorrow afternoon." I hung up the phone.

Two days later, late Tuesday morning, I stood in Cher's embrace on my front lawn. A teardrop splashed on the shoulder of my T-shirt. Cher, sniffling, slipped out of my hug, patting my shoulder once. She smiled at me, the light in her eyes dim like the invisible sun behind clouds at daybreak. She cupped my cheek in one hand. "Be good, kiddo." She sniffled again and climbed into the back seat of my parents' Grand Prix. I wiped a tear from my cheek.

"Well, that's that," Marie mumbled, spinning and vanishing into our house.

I wished I could drag my sister out of our house, shove her to the itchy, thick-bladed South Florida grass, shake her by the shoulders, and scream that a thousand of Marie wasn't worth one of Cher.

Instead, I rushed to my room, where I hid until the early afternoon. I pulled out the AC/DC album I'd been hiding under my bed, the one I'd bought with allowance money. I played the first song on it, "Highway to Hell," over and over and over. I couldn't hear whether

Marie had left the house yet, but I knew if she hadn't left already, she'd be gone soon.

When I came out of my room, she wasn't in her bedroom. She wasn't anywhere in the house. Nobody was home. I closed her bedroom door behind me and tore her beige and purple paradise upside down.

I started with her closet, searching in every shoe, every pocket, every shoe box and bag, every nook and cranny. I even pulled up the carpet, although the floor was concrete underneath.

I ripped through her vanity and her main dresser, pulling out the drawers and checking behind them, tugging the dresser away from the wall. Dropping down to check underneath. Still nothing. I shook her lamp to make sure the base wasn't hollow.

My sister used a second, smaller, low dresser as a night table beside her bed. On top of this dresser sat a beige, three-shelved bookcase. I emptied the case of every bauble and book, checking inside each book to make sure she hadn't cut a hiding space into the pages. Nothing, though. I left these items on her bed, and I threw my arms around the bookshelf and wriggled it forward on the dresser, at an angle so I could see behind it.

Jackpot!

A clear plastic baggie bursting with pot was secured by masking tape to the case's wooden back panel. Wherever Marie went yesterday afternoon, she bought more grass. That's what she did with the money she earned as a cashier at Peaches Records and Tapes. Bought weed.

I peeled off the masking tape and studied the plastic bag. I emptied half of it, maybe a little more than I needed, into the baggie I'd snagged from the kitchen. There were some pills in there, too, the little white ones, with 'RORER 714' printed in block letters. Quaaludes.

Those killed me.

I know, Shpresa. I'm not taking any pills. Even though I'm curious.

45

Don't.

I won't.

Also in the baggie was a slim pack of rolling papers and two crinkled twenty-dollar bills. I twirled one of the bills between my fingers.

Don't take that either. It's bad enough you're taking half her stash. She'll get you back, Steven. You're trying to get revenge on her, but she'll get revenge last. She's a snake, and snakes are best left alone if you can help it.

Let her try. Screw Marie.

Shpresa was silent.

I took one of the bills, shoving it into my pocket with my own half-filled baggie of pot.

Your funeral.

You're the one who had the funeral. Shh.

Not nice.

I taped the bag to the back panel and slid the bookcase in place. I arranged everything else in the room the way I found it. As if that mattered once Marie discovered what I'd done.

I stashed the grass under my mattress, and I took a long hot shower. I slipped into some shorts and a T-shirt Joey's dad had given me—all us kids. The shirt had an image of Mickey Mouse holding an American flag, shooting a bird, and saying 'Hey Iran!" The Ayatollah still had our hostages, after all. I'd hidden the shirt and never planned to wear it. Until now.

Nice shirt.

Joey's dad gave them to us. They're still holding our people hostage, and my parents are gonna be gone all day, so they won't see it.

Albanians. Iranians. They're all the same, right? So, fuck 'em all?

No. I didn't say that, Shpresa. Just Iran.

Hmm. Your shirt speaks for you.

46

I hopped on my bicycle and headed to Annie's.

Do. It.

The new girl sat on a wooden bar stool on the opposite side of the ping pong table from Peter's empty spot. Peter, his back to me as he played Billy in ping pong, stood in the garage entrance. *Annie must have pulled the extra stool from inside her house for her friend*, was my first thought. I don't know why that was the *first* thing that came to my mind. The second thing that popped into my brain, the most important thing, was that the new girl was cute. I had a poster of Linda Ronstadt taped above my bed, the photograph in which the singer wore a white orchid in her hair. The new girl, with her thick dark hair, pulled back by barrettes, and large dark brown eyes, looked like the singer. She wore a dark blue bikini top, cut-off light blue jean shorts, and white sandals, and everything about her was alright. The third thing I thought was that goshdarnit, Peter, with his thin angular face, high cheekbones, and deep tan, was more likely to catch her eye than me. She would go for him first.

I popped the kickstand on my Schwinn, parking it beside the Impala. I was strolling up the driveway as Billy, with a roar, smashed a volley past Peter and out of the garage. Maybe it was luck, maybe it was

48

God, maybe it was Shpresa guiding my reflexes, but as the small white ball zipped toward me, I stuck out my hand and snagged it, just like that, out of the air. The nifty catch made me appear about one thousand percent more athletic than I was. The new girl, who remained the focus of my attention, widened her eyes and smirked, a cute dimple forming on one of her cheeks. As if she wasn't already hot enough. "Nice catch," she murmured, locking eyes with me for one. Two. Three seconds. What was happening?

I tore my gaze from her and tossed the ball to Peter. "Your ball, dude."

Annie jumped up and rushed around the table, getting almost chest to chest with me. Like her friend, she wore cut-off jeans shorts and a bikini top, hers canary yellow. The mighty mite pressed up on her tip toes and tilted up her chin because I stood a few inches taller than her. But here she was, getting in my face, her bubble gum breath wafting into my nostrils, and her light brown eyes scorching me. Behind her, in the garage, the dark-haired new girl, who Peter said was named Sherry or Sheryl, frowned.

"You got something for me?" Annie asked.

"You two should fight," Peter muttered.

Screw you, Petey.

"I do have something for you." I tugged the baggie out of my pocket, almost dropping it on the asphalt, but keeping a loose hold. "Here." I extended it to her.

Her head swiveled as she scanned up and down the street, eyes darting about before she grabbed the contraband and shoved it into her pocket. "You came through. Good."

"I'm sorry."

"There was money in there. Why?"

"It's a twenty. Extra for the trouble I caused."

49

I glanced at Peter. The trouble Petey caused, too.

"Huh. Okay, I'll take it. Looks like good weed, too. More light-green than brown."

"I think it's sinsemilla. No seeds. Maui Wowie." There were no seeds or stems in what I'd taken from Marie; my sister must have sprung for the good stuff. But I made up that last part about the weed being Maui Wowie, which one of the older kids in our neighborhood once claimed was the best strain of pot.

"Alright then." Annie spun and returned to her chair. Before she sat, she slapped Billy's butt as he was about to serve.

"Stop," he grumbled half seriously, shooting her a brooding look with his dark, expressive eyebrows.

I entered the garage, standing on the side where the new girl sat, keeping a couple of feet between her and me. "What's the score?"

"15–10, me," Billy replied as he served an ace to Peter. "16–10. Hah!"

I felt the weight of the new girl's gaze, so I glanced at her, prepared to give her a weak smile. She was staring at the table, though, as if her eyes had been glued to the game the whole time. I could have sworn she was looking at me a moment before. Did she look away that quickly?

"This is Sharon," Annie poked her chin at me. "Sharon, this is dickwad. I mean, this is Stevie."

Everybody laughed, including the new girl.

That was pretty funny.

I'll admit, Shpresa, it was funny.

The new girl smiled at me, dimples forming on each cheek, the kind of smile that lights a room and makes you forget there could be heaven and hell. Her teeth were white and straight, lips full and bowed, and her dimples were like tiny angelic indents under each cheekbone. Her smile sent me falling, falling, falling. "Hey, Stevie." She spoke with sort of a high pitch, a touch raspy.

"Hey." I gulped, hoping the lump caught in my throat wasn't too noticeable. She smirked. "You going into eleventh?" I asked her, dreading she would say 'yes.'

"Tenth. I'll be fifteen in mid-October."

Good God above! My mother was right. Jesus was real, and he was watching over me! Sharon was only a grade ahead of me, not two grades like Annie. *And* she was young for her grade, only about half-a-year older than me.

"What grade are you going into?"

"Uh, I'm turning fifteen a few months after you." I felt like it was important to make that point first, that she was only five to six months older than me. "But, uh, I'm going into ninth at Oakland Park High."

"Stevie's real book smart. Like Robbie Sheldon."

"Oh, yeah? Maybe we'll have class together next year at OP."

Oh, God, if only.

Steven, breathe. Calm your palpitating heart or you're going to pass out.

Shh. Leave me alone, Shpresa.

My heart *was* racing, and my palms were sweating because Annie's garage was a sticky oven. As if to confirm how hot it was, a bead of sweat trickled from Sharon's temple and down her cheek and neck, pooling in the notch at the base of her neck. I was mesmerized by it, and almost reached out and wiped it off. Thank God, I caught myself and did not.

Relax. Be yourself.

What does that even mean, Shpresa? What if I'm an asshole? Should I still be me?

Billy whooped—another victory cry. He'd won another point. Another three points? Four points?

"Did you have Algebra this year?" I asked her. "I'll be in Algebra II next year."

"Yeah." She smiled again, and it was like somebody lit a lantern at the prow of a ship, casting its glow upon the shore of a tropical paradise. I could even smell the papaya, or maybe that was her shampoo, conditioner, or skin cream. "That'd be cool if we were in Algebra II together." She swallowed once, hard. Was she nervous, too? "Where'd you get the good weed?" she asked.

"My sister."

Annie interrupted our deep conversation. "Sharon ain't never got high before. Neither has Stevie. You're both goody-goodies. Maybe we'll smoke a j later."

It wasn't true that I'd never smoked, but Annie calling me a goody-goody made me think of Cher. Marie had called my cousin a goody-goody when she first moved in with us. Sometime over the last year Marie had stopped calling Cher that, maybe when she discovered our cousin had sex with Sal, her ex-boyfriend, and got pregnant. Got an abortion. My shoulders slumped as I thought about how, right about now—or maybe it had already happened—Cher was exiting my parents' car and hauling her duffle bag into some creepy facility at The Sprout where the staff would be mean to her.

"You okay?" Sharon asked, her large, dark brown eyes narrowing.

My face must have been showing all my feelings, and I tried my best to wipe the sadness off it. "Yeah. It's just…my cousin's going to a drug rehab today." I glanced at Peter, who focused on his serve, concentrating on the game in front of him. "She didn't deserve it, is all. She's cool."

"I'm sorry." Sharon sounded genuinely sorry for my cousin.

I glanced at Annie, who made a grunting sound and glared at Peter, who, uncharacteristically, served into the net. Did Annie suspect Peter helped steal her grandmother's pot?

"Game!" yelled Billy, snapping his fingers and jabbing an index finger at Peter. "Dude, you suck."

Annie giggled, and I bit my bottom lip trying not to smile.

Peter handed me the peeling green paddle. "You're in the back, Stevie. He's on fire today. See if you can do better."

"We're headed to Robbie's, now," Annie proclaimed. Rob Sheldon, his house built on an oversized corner lot, was the only kid with a swimming pool on our street at the far end of the neighborhood.

"Not now. Stevie's gotta play Billy first," Peter whined.

Peter wants Billy to humiliate you in front of Sharon.

I know. I'll try to play well though.

Annie stood. "No, let's go to Rob's now. He said his parents get home at six and it's two thirty. I called him earlier, and I told him we'd come swim before his folks got home."

Annie called Rob Sheldon on the phone? Or was she saying this to get me out of this game with Billy.

It's the little things, Shpresa whispered, *that make a friendship.*

What does that mean, Shpresa?

Annie grabbed the paddle out of my hands. "Sharon can ride on your handlebars, Stevie." Peter was standing beside me as she said this, and I could feel his head explode.

"Cool," murmured Sharon, and my chest swelled with the hope that this might be a good day.

About a half-hour later, we played the game Marco Polo, swimming and running around Rob's pool. Annie sidled up to me as she and I hung onto the pool's edge in the deep end. She whispered into my ear, "Sharon told me she likes you. She thinks yer cute."

53

My breath got stuck in my chest. "Really?" I caught Sharon's smile and twinkling eyes from the other side of the pool.

"I hooked you up. That's for giving me an extra twenty dollars and sayin' you was sorry. Did you pay your sister for that grass?"

Annie was forgiving me easily. "Nope."

Billy, his eyes squeezed shut, waist deep in the shallow end, was 'it.'

"Marco!"

"Polo!"

Billy made a swooping dive toward the deep end, swimming underwater and waving his arms wildly to tag someone. Annie dipped underwater, and I followed her down, wiggling like a snake past unsuspecting Billy, emerging on the other side of the pool where Sharon had been holding onto the lip of the pool. Except, she was gone now.

Annie tilted her head, fiddled her pinky inside her ear, and whispered to me again. "You like to pay your sister if yer smart, Stevie. I wouldn't mess around with that chick."

Did Annie know Marie? Before Annie dropped out, she and Marie had been in the same grade at Oakland Park High, so I supposed it made sense. Also, who did Annie think she was, giving me advice? She wasn't Shpresa. I had enough money to pay back my sister, maybe sixty-something dollars stashed under my bed, what remained of my allowance for chores. But I was not planning to pay her because I was mad about Cher. "Marie had it coming. She won't narc." I sounded like my mom as I said she had it coming.

"Hmm. Hey, Sharon's going inside the house now. Go in after her to use Rob's bathroom."

"What?"

"Do as I say. Go after her!"

"Fish out of water!"

"I lose," Sharon said with a light laugh, a white and dark-blue striped beach towel wrapped around her waist as she tiptoed across the burning hot, pebbled patio. She squinted at me for a split second, rolled open the slider with a rumble, and vanished into Rob's house.

"Go!" Annie shoved my shoulder.

Go.

I climbed out of the pool, splashing as I went.

"Fish out of water!"

"I lose, too," I muttered, forgetting to grab a towel and pat myself off before I rushed through the open slider. Sharon was coming out of the bathroom as I dripped down the tiled hallway.

Did she really go to the bathroom so quickly?

Rob's hallway was narrow and dark, the house quiet and empty. "Hey, Stevie," she said. At first, I thought she was going to sidle by me and continue down the narrow hall to his family room off the pool. I even politely turned sideways a little to let her pass, smiling as she approached and slowed her pace. Slowed. She slowed, and the world switched to slow motion. She stopped. I might have stopped breathing again.

"Hey, Stevie."

She stood about a foot from me. Close.

"Hey, Sharon."

Step forward. One step.

Okay.

I stepped toward her. Our eyes locked. She was maybe an inch taller than Annie, still shorter than me, and her face, inches from mine, tilted up as she strained onto her tiptoes, her hands warm on the back of my damp neck. Her hands on my neck? Was this happening?

Our mouths came closer together, and our lips touched. Brushed against each other. She sucked on my bottom lip, pressed her soft mouth harder into mine. Her mouth opened, and it was déjà vu all over again, my mind sparking like a firework fuse and exploding in a shower of colors as her tongue swirled, wet and warm, around my tongue. Her wet bikini top was plastered against me, the softness of her breasts pressing on my bare chest. She combed her fingertips through my wet hair, and my trembling fingertips gripped each side of her waist above the towel, her skin there dry but cool.

"Grab my butt," she whispered.

"What?"

"Underneath. With both hands. It's hard to stand on my toes like this, so hold me up. Here, like this." She took my hands and placed them over the fuzzy towel, under the soft cushion of each of her butt cheeks, where they folded over above her legs. I could feel the outline of her bikini through the wet towel, and I squeezed a little, wondering if I was allowed to do that. She didn't tell me to stop, so I did it some more. We continued to kiss, and her hand worked its way down my ribs, and I shivered. And—

"Dude! What the hell? Steven, you made a mess in my hall. The floor's got puddles!" Rob, his face screwed up like a prune, marched down his hallway. Sharon and I broke apart. He made no acknowledgment that he'd caught us making out, only shouted again about water on his hallway floor.

"Sorry. Uh, good thing it's not carpet. I'll get a towel and wipe it."

"Do it!" Rob barked as he edged past us and disappeared into his bathroom.

Sharon and I looked at each other. She giggled once, and we both burst out laughing.

"Do! It!" shouted Rob, his voice muffled from inside his bathroom.

Sharon unwrapped her towel, knelt, and wiped the ground with it. "Do! It!" she mocked in a low voice, offering me an adorable smirk, and we both laughed again.

"I heard that," shouted Rob from behind the door.

"We're doing it, Rob. Relax. Can I help you with that, Sharon? It's my fault."

She rose, clutching my forearm to tug herself up. "No, I'm done. Come on." She grabbed my hand, lacing her fingers in mine. "Annie's a good driver. She drove me over here from Palm Aire. That's where I live. My parents don't know she doesn't have her license yet."

"Oh." I didn't know what to say. Why would Sharon tell me that random fact?

"Annie's getting her driver's license the Saturday after next. We're going to the movies. Our friend, Dave Wonka, is an usher at Movie City 11, and he's gonna let us sneak into *Friday the Thirteenth*."

"Oh. Isn't that rated R?"

"Uh, huh. It's gonna be cool."

"Cool."

She's inviting you to the movies, dumbass.

"You can go, right?"

"Uh, yeah." If my mom lets me. "I'll have to tell my mom I'm seeing something else."

"Duh." Sharon squeezed my hand. She dragged the slider, which shuddered open, and waved toward the pool deck. "Gentlemen first."

"You've got age *and* beauty on me." I don't know why I said that, but I immediately regretted it because it sounded so dumb.

But she smiled at my comment, kept her hand out, like 'proceed,' and said, "Do. It."

I chuckled, accepted her chivalry, and stepped onto the pool deck.

The Hangar and the Horror

Saturday, June 28, 1980

"Are we done here?" I asked, hoping my voice didn't quaver. Marie's mattress gave a little as I rose from it.

My sister, icy blue eyes stabbing me, dropped a hand to my shoulder and not so gently pressed me back to her bed. "Is that really how you want to play it, Steven?"

I swallowed hard. She kept her hand, a lead weight, on my shoulder. She and I hadn't gotten into a physical fight since I got taller than her almost two years ago and she stopped picking on me. But she wasn't that much smaller than me either; she'd inherited our mom's Swedish genes, and she was athletic, with a powerful gymnast's frame. I wasn't sure if clumsy little me would come out on top if we came to blows. Even so, I swiped at her hand, knocking it from my shoulder. She laid her tanned hand right back on me. "You really don't want to do this, Steven." I grabbed her hand, and pried it from my shoulder, maybe squeezing it too hard. She cocked back her right hand in a fist and sucked in her bottom lip like she was about to sock me. On instinct,

58

my hands whipped up in front of my face, making her laugh. "You're such a pussy."

"What's wrong with you, Marie? I told you, fair's fair."

"Fair is not fair. I gave you almost two weeks, Steven, and now you're refusing to do what's right. I told you that was my stuff. You owe me."

"You set up Cher. She's our cousin, and you messed her over," I hissed, repeating the accusation I'd leveled at her moments before, what I'd been wanting to say for almost the last two weeks. I clenched and unclenched my fists, my jaw tensing, my face warming. Why, oh why, when I got mad, did my eyes start to burn and tears squeak from them, threatening to make me feel weak? My bottom lip trembled, and I wiped at my eye.

She laughed again, her blonde hair bouncing lightly as her shoulders shook with delight. "Oh, my God, are you gonna squirt some? Go on, Baby Huey, squirt some tears." Her laughter dried up, and she jabbed her middle finger a sliver away from my nose. "If you do not give me my grass and my money back, you will regret it for the rest of your short life, Steven. I am the hammer, and you are the nail. And my hammer will drop on you."

A light honk, then another honk out front of our house split the dim, early morning silence. Our heads swung toward her front bedroom window.

"That's my ride. Have fun with mom and dad at The Sprout today." She waggled her fingers as she grabbed a canvas bag from the corner of her room. "Sing some songs to God for me."

She exited her room whistling the tune to "Greensleeves."

I checked her clock. Seven in the morning. The faint smell of bacon wafted from the other side of the house. My mom was making breakfast like she said she would. We were going to see Cher for the first time in almost two weeks, and I had no idea what to expect. All I knew was it made my stomach turn flips to think about going to that place.

Make it through the morning, Steven. Be very, very, very quiet. Tell them nothing. Later, you'll go to the movies with Sharon, and everything will be okay.

Tell them nothing? What are they going to ask me?

Tell them nothing. You'll see.

A small outpost. A wood-paneled office disguised as a tiny, two-room log cabin. My parents and I sat on metal folding chairs, the kind pro wrestlers beat each other with, or the kind of chair that might be used at a church social. An attractive young man—maybe in his mid-to-late twenties, with a thin dark mustache, very dark slicked-back hair, and looking vaguely like the singer Freddie Mercury from Queen—slid through a door in the back of the office. He wore gray slacks, a white shirt, and a solid dark gray tie. Slick, starched, and pressed to perfection. He leaned over the monstrous wooden desk that separated him from us, shook my parents' hands, aimed a punchy nod at me, and sat in a cushioned armchair behind the desk. A woman—also youngish, wearing a dress that reminded me of something Cher would wear, periwinkle with a yellow floral pattern, her long, light brown hair disappearing behind her shoulders, straight against her back—entered through the same door and sat beside him. A tiny gold cross hung from a chain around the woman's neck as if mimicking the cross hanging over my mother's cream blouse.

I closed my eyes in a vain attempt to contain and dissolve the nausea building in my stomach.

The woman didn't shake my parents' hands, nor did she look at me. "Mr. Jacobs. Mrs. Jacobs. Good to see you again. Mr. Carnavale can't make it this morning, but he sends his regards," she said.

"How is Cher doing?" my dad asked, nudging his gold-rimmed glasses to the bridge of his longish nose, and seeming genuinely concerned.

The man cleared his throat. "She's doing quite well. I think everything will work out for her. She seems to be in a good place, with a solid base to grow into a flower. She truly wants to rid her life of bad influences. She's nearly ready for the second step." He smoothed his dark tie and folded his arms across his chest.

Something about the way the man said 'nearly ready' made my skin crawl. It felt like he wanted to say there was something big holding Cher back, something making her unworthy in their eyes, but he wasn't voicing it. I'd heard enough double talk from people at church to tease that from his words and tone.

"Good," answered my mom, not noticing the untruthfulness in his language and demeanor.

The young woman considered me with dead eyes, and my stomach performed maybe a half-dozen more somersaults. Her gaze reminded me of the blank, thousand-yard stare Julie Johnson had given me in church. Except her stare was more in control, like a Death Star laser beam burning through me and slicing into my soul. If churchgoer Cynthia Johnson's daughter Julie was a robot, this woman was the lead robot, an automaton disguised as a human. "You must be Steven."

"Uh, yes."

A whiff of lavender wafted under my nose. I assumed it was her perfume. "I'm Rebeccah. How are you today?"

"Uh, fine."

"What do you like to do for fun, Steven?"

Careful. Careful. Say very little.

"I, uh, like to hang with my friends."

She shifted in her seat, but her expression remained serene. "And what do you and your friends like to do for fun?"

"We, uh, play ping pong. Swim. Play Marco Polo. Bicycle."

Those eyes, like they were tractor beams, sucked in the information I spit out. "And what else do you like to do?"

"Uh, read. My friend Rob has a computer. It's called an Apple III. It's his dad's really. I think his dad was involved in creating it or something. Or he knows somebody who made it."

"Computer." The woman said the word softly but also as if the word left a bad taste in her mouth. "Apple you say. We should be careful with apples, right? Like in Eden." She smiled. But it wasn't really a smile. It was something else.

"Steven is very bright," my mother interjected.

"I can see that. What types of books do you like to read, Steven?"

Goosepimples crept up the flesh of my arms, and my hands grew cold. I could feel my heart beating in my ears. Why was she asking me so many questions? Did my sister narc on me? Did my parents bring me here so they could take me in as a sprout? I blinked back tears, sniffed.

Don't let them see you're upset, Steven. Don't let them see. They feed on it.

"I like to read. Uh, I read Narnia. And, uh, *A Wrinkle in Time*."

"Narnia." Again, she said it like she wanted to spit. "We need to protect ourselves from books masquerading as the truth of the Lord. I don't know the wrinkle book. It sounds…sciencey." Again, she seemed like she wanted to gargle with some mouthwash after saying the word sciencey. "Do you read the Bible, Steven?"

"Uh, sometimes. At church." I scratched my neck where it met my collarbone beneath the V-collar of my burnt-orange velour shirt.

"What's your favorite verse?"

Thank God, I knew a verse, or I sort of knew one. "He is able to exceed abundance above all that we ask or think, with the power that works in us." I hoped I didn't screw it up too badly.

She nodded. "Ephesians 3:20 is a powerful verse. I suppose your version is good enough for today. Now unto Him that is able to do exceedingly abundantly above all that we ask or think, according to the power that worketh in us. Do you know what it means?"

My mind froze. I blanked and stared at her like I was mute.

"It means God has the glory because he can do so much more within us than we could imagine Him doing. Like he can rid us of desires to rebel. The desire to rebel instead of obeying leads us to weed and pills. And soon you're in the ghetto shooting up heroin."

Ghetto? Rebel. Heroin? For some reason, an image from *A Wrinkle in Time* popped into my head: children bouncing red rubber balls in time with each other. Obeying their dark master. I thought I read somewhere that L'Engle was a Christian. I kept my mouth shut about that.

"What music do you listen to Steven?"

My dad crossed and uncrossed his legs beside me. He checked his watch.

No! For Christ's sake, don't say that!

I was about to say AC/DC and Van Halen, but Shpresa saved me. If I'd answered "Highway to Hell" and "Running with the Devil," I might as well have packed my bags.

"Debby Boone," I said, the first thing that popped into my head. I think my mom liked Debby Boone, who seemed wholesome to me. The song, "You Light Up My Life," came to mind.

You light up my life, too, Steven.

Ha, ha, Shpresa. Nothing's funny here.

I bit back a smirk.

63

The woman tilted her head just slightly. "Do your friends smoke cigarettes, Steven?"

"No," I snapped, maybe a bit too quickly, thinking of Annie's Marlboros.

"It's almost time for group. Are you ready to go in and be a part, Steven? Even if you're in the audience, you're a part of the whole."

"Okay." My reply came as an obedient whisper, and everyone stood as if on cue, and they ushered us out the office's back door. We passed down a covered, fenced-in footpath that led to the door of the jet-plane-sized hangar I'd spied as my dad had swung our car into the gravel lot. The hangar was cavernous inside. Big enough to fit a jet, but most of it was quiet, empty space. People—teenagers—sat in two rows of folding chairs facing the door we entered. There were seven chairs in each row, with one empty chair, so I counted thirteen sprouts. I wondered where the fourteenth teen was. Cher sat in the front row, and my heart jumped. She spotted me; her mouth trembled as if she wanted to smile but invisible fingers were poking and prodding at her lips. I offered her a forced and wary smile with my lips pressed together. She answered me with tired eyes, deep dark crescents beneath them.

Like she was smushed. *Oh, Cher. God, I'm so sorry, Cher.*

We sat in the front row of chairs about twenty feet across from the teens. Cher, wearing blue jeans and a light-yellow sweater, dropped her gaze to her sneakers, and I did the same. The enormous room was quiet for some time. After studying my shoes for what seemed like hours, I lifted my gaze to the high, curved ceiling of the hangar. Did regrets drift to the top and get stuck there like helium-filled balloons? I dropped my eyes to my sneakers again.

As I inspected my laces, Shpresa spoke. *They've been keeping her in an isolated room down the hall from the others. Forcing her to stay up all night, playing Christmas Carols loud on a stereo. Yelling at her. Telling her she's no good. Then telling her how good they think she really is. Then telling her she's no good again. Giving her a little food and water. More yelling at her. More Christmas music. Letting her weep. Comforting her. Letting her get an hour of sleep if she tells them what they want to hear. Then telling her they know she's the good one in her family, she was led astray. Teaching her chants, twisted versions of nursery rhymes, to remind herself to stay away from all evildoers when she gets back to the real world. Asking her, over and over and over, which person in the house was in on it. Asking whether it's you or your sister who shared those drugs with her. Two baggies. They know there was someone else. Tell them, and she'll get what she needs. Slapping her lightly on the cheek or a little harder on the top of her head—what they call taps of love. Telling her they love her, that's why they're being hard on her. Threatening her with worse. If she doesn't like their love taps, claiming she can simply head off to juvie where the tough girls will stick a broomstick up her, and I quote Rebeccah, 'up her hoo-hah.' Or up her butt. But Cher hasn't broken yet, Steven. Not yet. Maybe she never will. But they're threatening her with six months living in the barracks instead of two months if she doesn't come clean about her accomplice. She's hanging on. But just barely.*

God. They're going to get me. I rubbed my sweaty palms on my shorts and tried to control my breathing. I swallowed down the bile inching its way up my throat.

In my mind, I said a prayer to the real God for Cher: *Please protect my cousin.* A real God wouldn't let her be punished for this, like she was nothing to nobody. *Please protect her, Jesus.*

You're a good cousin, Steven. And it's okay, maybe they won't get you. You did good today with Rebeccah; your answers were good enough. She's Howel's right-hand woman. She thinks you're nothing more than a big dork. Later this evening, when she sneaks away from the barracks and heads to the bar for a bourbon…or three or four…and picks herself out a violent one-night stand with some random mustache, as she's slipping back into her satin hot pants in the very early morning, she'll think of you vaguely. She'll remember what a spaz you are. How it's probably your sister who's the better sprout candidate, not you. Even though she believes you would break easier.

How do you know this?

I don't really. Know this. I'm imagining it. Maybe you know it. Maybe you can sense it. Steven?

Yes, Shpresa.

These are bad people, Steven. Take care. Say very little each time. They want you to come into the barracks. They want you to sit in the front row as a sprout in this massive, hollow airplane hangar. You or your sister. They don't care which of you comes in as long as they can get one of you. Since the lawsuit, their program has shrunk. That's why Howel has told Rebeccah and her friend, Freddie Mercury, whatever his name is, to get a confession from Cher. They want bodies. They want another body. They have fascist vampire hearts, and they need to suck on fresh blood.

Why?

Money.

Money?

Yes, money. Your father took a second mortgage to put Cher in here. You heard him talking to the bank.

I did.

So, you sort of know about the money. Oh, they've started singing. Go on, you're supposed to sing with them. After the singing, Cher will stand and share with the group what an enormous druggie she is and why it's great she's in this place. Wonderful.

I raised my eyes. Cher was singing to the tune of "Greensleeves" along with the other twelve teens, her gaze not at me but through me. Beside me, my mom fumbled with the song's words, and on the other side of me, an older, heavy, balding man I didn't know, I assumed somebody's parent, almost shouted the words like he'd been here many times before:

> The Sprout, no doubt
> Is all about
> Washing the weed and the pills right out
> Get up each day from dawn past dusk
> The branch of the Sprout
> Is what we trust
> And if we fail
> We will not shout
> We'll scrub ourselves harder
> To get the stain out

Nausea, burbling inside my gut since my conversation with Rebeccah, rumbled up, overwhelming me. I sprang up, and I rushed toward the tiny bathroom I'd spied on the way in, my hand over my mouth, bile bubbling again into my throat. Slamming the bathroom door behind me. Kneeling and disgorging my fear, anger, frustration, and sorrow into the perfectly polished bowl. Vomiting a thick spray again and again. Vile light brown liquid and chunks. Fearful all the while that they might think I was puking because I was a druggie.

A drip of brown vomit had found its way to the front of my shirt, darkening the fabric. I leaned my forearms on the toilet seat, my head facedown almost inside the smelly bowl, knowing I'd need to head back to the folding chairs soon before Cher started to speak. Make a good show of it for all of them.

Come on, Steven. Up with you. Wipe your mouth. Clean off your shirt. Get the stain out.

Get the stain out.

Billy popped the top on the Cool Mule beer and flicked the tab out the passenger-side window. He reached into the backseat and handed Sharon the beer. He opened another and handed the can back to me. He opened a third beer and extended it to Annie, her hands gripping the steering wheel. Annie, who was focused on driving her grandmother's beast of a car, shook her head at him. He kept the beer for himself, taking three enormous gulps. He wiped his mouth. "God damn, that movie was the best!" he declared, then belched.

Annie kept her eyes on the road. "Gross."

"It was," I agreed. I imitated the music that had played every time the killer was about to claim their victim, chh-chh-chh-ki-ki-ki or something like that, and everybody laughed.

Sharon's warm hand was folded into mine, her thumb caressing my palm. With her other hand, she sipped on her beer as she stared out the window. "Ugh. Billy, this beer is so bad. Couldn't you have bought Miller beer?"

I took a sip. Sharon was right. "It is pretty bad."

"Dude, screw both of you. Cool Mule Beer is ninety-nine cents a six-pack!" Billy laughed.

Exactly.

Sharon leaned forward. "Where are we going, Annie?"

"To the beach. A good spot. Private. But don't have sex there."

"Why not?" Billy asked Annie seriously, with no hint of irony in his voice.

Annie smirked at him. "Ain't you learned nothing from that movie? If we have sex, the killer'll chop us to pieces."

Sharon laughed weakly as if she was nervous.

"I'll kick his ass." Billy puffed his chest.

Kick her ass.

Shh, Shpresa. No spoilers.

We passed over the bubble of a bridge spanning the intercoastal. Annie's grandmother's car wound through back roads behind condominiums on the other side. We parked somewhere behind the tall buildings and hustled across A1A to the beach. On the sidewalk on the other side of the street, we took off our shoes, holding them as we headed onto the beach. The smell of salt drifted into my nose, and the gentle waves stroking the shore broke through the noise of traffic as our feet hit the dry sand. The air was thick and warm, even at night. Typical for South Florida.

Annie was right, it was dark and quiet in this beach spot above the water. Annie and Billy strolled down toward the ocean, the darkness swallowing them. Sharon and I sort of half-sat, half-leaned against an overturned rowboat on the dry sand, closer to the street than the ocean but still cloaked in shadows. "Wanna go walk down by the water?"

She shook her head. "No, let's stay here. Are you okay?"

"What?"

"We've hung out together like a bunch of times now."

"Yeah." Every time, we'd been either at Annie's or, a couple of times, at Rob's pool.

"You've been quieter tonight than before. Are you nervous because it's our first date? We held hands in the movie. I like being with you, and you're a good kisser." With this, she pecked me on the lips. "For a freshman."

You can tell her how you're feeling. And why.

I can? Thank God.

I sighed, releasing tense, hot energy from my midsection. "I like you, too, Sharon. Uh, you kiss great, too. It's just...it's my cousin. I can't stop thinking about her."

"The one in rehab. Are you like in love with her?" Her voice came out a little hard.

Why would she think that? "Oh, no. No. She's my first cousin. That would be incest. I'm not from Alabama. No. I just care about her."

"Oh. Then, what is it?"

"We went to The Sprout today. My parents and me. To see her."

"Oh. You were inside there?" Her voice was filled with awe, maybe a hint of fear.

"Yeah, we were in this big hangar up the road from their barracks, the living quarters. My cousin looked tired. I don't think they're treating her good. And they think either my sister or me is a druggie. They want to get one of us in there, I think."

"Oh."

I wanted to tell her how I threw up. But I didn't. "It was super creepy."

"What did your sister think of it?"

"She didn't have to go. She went out fishing on her friend Helen's boat in the ocean."

"Your sister Marie gets away with stuff all the time, doesn't she? My brother's like that. So, I know."

I nodded.

"Last year, I saw Marie in the halls. Annie and your sister have the same dealer, but Annie told me to stay away from Marie. I didn't know she was your sister when I met you, but Annie told me after. Marie doesn't look much like you. You've got sandy brown hair, and it's kind of thin."

"Gee, thanks."

"No, no, I like it. But your sister's got all that thick, blonde hair like a movie star."

"I know. She got my mom's blonde hair."

"Your sister ruled the school, even in tenth grade."

I scoffed. "Try living with her."

Sharon inched closer to me, brushing my nose with hers in the sticky dark. "Let's stop talking about her."

"Okay."

Our lips met, and we kissed. Playfully. Slowly. Enjoying the tiny movements of each other's lips. Her breath tasting like peppermint. The warmth of her fingertips grazing my cheek. My thumb resting on her earlobe. The moisture on the tip of her tongue transferring to mine. Her soft hip giving beneath my hand.

She took a heavy breath as she broke away from the kiss. "We can't have sex here."

I jerked my head back. Did she notice me getting excited? Is that why she said something? "I–I didn't think—"

"If we have sex, a killer will get us." She grinned, and we both chuckled. "But we can do something else," she said.

"Oh. What?"

"Here, let me show you," she said, reaching for my zipper.

And she did. Show me.

And we did.

The full moon was a swollen white Quaalude above us, bathing us in its soft, mesmerizing glow. Hypnotizing us. I forgot about my troubles for a while. There was only the moon and Sharon. Sharon and the shimmering moon. After a while, I wasn't sure which was which.

Wang!

Monday, June 30, 1980

Rob and I scuttled between the grayish-white hills, which loomed like burial mounds beside the chalky water of the rock pit. In the early morning silence, the ashy piles of dirt and rock assumed a solemn stature. I half expected some Aboriginal tribe, like the people in Australia whom I'd read about in my *Encyclopedia Britannica*, to march around one of the larger mounds carrying a dead warrior's body, all dressed up in feathers, prepared for burial.

You need to go back and read a little more of that encyclopedia, Steven. That is not how it works. I think you're making stuff up in your head.

"Shh." Oh, shoot. I'd spoken to Shpresa out loud.

"I didn't say anything, dumbass. Who are you shushing?" One of Rob's favorite words was dumbass. Or maybe that was his favorite word when he was around me.

"I wasn't shushing you. I was about to say shoot. Like shhhoot. I forgot, uh, I'm supposed to meet Sharon later. Never mind."

Marvelous cover, Steven. That story made almost no sense.

72

It was an okay story.

I suppose.

Rob furrowed his brows. "Uh, huh. Sure."

We approached the break in the chain link fence on the other side of the rock pit. One broad wall of the high school came into view, a painting of a large green and black snake, fangs out, stretched across its face. The Vipers of Oakland Park High School took no prisoners. The kids called it OP High.

"How many more days of this?" I asked Rob as he peeled back the fence so I could slide through the gap.

"It's June thirtieth, so that's one week we've been going. It's a five-week session that goes to August first, so," Rob clucked five times, "Twenty-four more days after today. Wait, we're off this Friday for July fourth. Twenty-three days. Twenty-three days of lifting and sleeping behind the wrestling mats." He yawned. "Which is where I'm headed. To hide behind the mats and take a nap. I'm beat."

I pulled the fencing out toward me as Rob ducked and popped through the hole. "What are you doing later after gym?" I asked him. I don't know why I asked him this; it wasn't like I was planning to hang out with him later. Our physical education sessions at the high school went from eight to twelve noon, and since I'd met Sharon, I'd spent most afternoons at Annie's.

"Why, so you all can come over and bogart on my pool?"

He's on to you.

I shrugged. "Nah."

"A friend's coming over to my house. Glenn. He knows you from gifted."

"Glenn Austin?"

"Yep."

"How do you know him?" Rob, a year older than me, was going to be a sophomore at a magnet high school up in Delray Beach.

"I've been taking this free summer math course one night a week. It's good practice for the PSAT. It's over on Oakland Park Boulevard. It's something my dad signed me up for. He finds these crazy things. Glenn's in it even though the PSAT is two years away for him. Anyway, he and I were talking about computers, and he's coming over today to look at my dad's Apple III. I gotta go meet him near Oakland Park Boulevard after this."

I was stuck back on Rob's comment that he was somehow taking a free math course. And Rob was studying for the PSAT a year early? Over the summer? I wondered what kind of math it was. "Why are you meeting Glenn on Oakland Park Boulevard?"

"To walk with him to our neighborhood. He says cops sometimes bug him if he rides his bike anywhere north of there."

"Why?"

Rob scoffed, but he didn't answer me.

Because Glenn is Black, Steven. He's a young Black guy riding a bike. When the police see Glenn, they don't see an honors student at OP Middle. They don't treat him the way they treat you or Rob.

Oh. Ohhhh.

"Yeah, I get it."

We approached the gigantic mural of the viper, its fangs looming over us. We rounded the corner and headed toward the school's back courtyard. There, a sleepy gym teacher would take attendance before disappearing and leaving about twenty or so of us teens to our own devices. "Do you think our dads talked to each other about signing us up for this gym class?" I asked Rob.

Rob cocked his head. "Dude, you don't know how it went down?"

"Know what?"

"Your dad came over to my house back in May. I heard him talking with my dad in the den. They're trying to keep you away from Peter and Billy. Trying to keep me away from them, too, I guess, though good luck with me having a pool. They're trying to keep us away from Joey Bucci, except they don't know he's not even around this summer. They probably wish this gym class went all day from eight to five."

We were whispering in the line-up in the school's back courtyard, against a paddleball wall.

"Why would they want to do that?"

"Our dads don't like these kids. They don't like their parents either. Peter's dad is in the mob or something. Who knows what he does, really? They don't like Joey's older brother, Sal. Billy has a rep. Blah blah. Your dad came to my dad because they're both ex-Navy. So now I'm stuck in this thing with you."

Did Rob blame me for being here in this summer gym class?

He continued. "I don't even get high school credit for this. My dad thought it would be good for me to lift weights every morning and because it's free." Rob patted his own bicep. "So, I guess it's useful. I'm going out for football next year. Offensive line."

Football? Brainy Rob Sheldon? Huh. "Aren't most linemen like huge?" Rob wasn't much taller than me, maybe five-eight or five-nine, although he was built solidly, thick.

Rob shrugged as we filed into the weight room with about a dozen or so other guys who didn't stay outside to play basketball. There were only two girls in the class, and they could be found sitting on the tennis courts chatting most of the morning.

Inside the spacious, high-ceiling weight room, off in one corner, a muscled boy—young man—leaned over a long bar with a forty-five-pound weight on each end. He was about six feet tall, with light-brown skin and curly dark hair, and he wore a thin-strapped tank top that might as well have been spray painted onto his swollen, chiseled form. A leather weight belt was cinched around his midsection like it was trapping air in his upper torso, making his upper-body muscles bigger. A bunch of beefy guys gathered around him, chanting, "Wang! Wang! Wang! Wang!" His biceps and shoulder muscles swelled even more as he took a fierce underhand grip on the bar.

"Dude, he's gonna curl one-hundred thirty-five pounds a bunch of times. He's in eleventh grade. Wang is a beast!"

"You know him?" The older boy's face had stretched into a grimace as if he was practicing suffering *before* he lifted the weights off the ground.

"I don't know him. I heard about him. He's Scott Wang, Oakland Park's star linebacker."

"He wasn't here the other days. Is he in this gym class?"

"No, he must have come here just to lift. Some of those guys over there aren't in this class either. They must be OP varsity football players. My high school plays them next year, but I'll probably be JV.

Wang, the veins on his arms, chest, and neck bulging as if they were trying to pop out of his skin, heaved up the bar with a mighty growl. He curled the massive amount once, twice, three, four times before dropping it with a thud, the round plates bouncing on the rubber mat at his feet.

Meanwhile, Rob, presumably motivated by the presence of Wang, had not, as usual, scurried next door to the wrestling room to curl up and snooze behind a mat. Instead, he'd set himself up with the same weight arrangement, but on the bench press, a bar with a forty-five-pound weight on each end—it was much easier to bench press that amount than curl it. Knowing my place, I walked behind the bench to spot my friend—to make sure he didn't injure or kill himself by dropping the weight on his chest.

In the corner, the OP football dudes still cheered and clapped Wang on the back, some of them still repeating, Wang! Wang! Wang!

High school gods.

Before Rob laid his shoulders onto the bench, he did his head-cocking thing again and said, "We can be anything we want to be, Steve. Believe it." He cleared his throat. "Sorry about your cousin, man. She got a raw deal." I had told him that Cher went into The Sprout, but not the details.

"Thanks." This was a switch from his usual snippy demeanor.

Rob found his grip, and I readied myself to help lift off the bar for him.

"Come over and hang with Glenn and me later." He breathed hard twice in preparation for the lift.

I was supposed to meet Sharon and Annie at Billy's that afternoon. Billy's parents were gone.

Say okay. Go to Rob's house instead.

"Okay. I'll come over." I lifted the bar.

Sharon's voice sounded tinny on the line, very far away. "You could have called Billy's house."

"We got caught up looking at Rob's dad's computer. I meant to get down there. Uh, sorry."

I should have called her.

Eh. Shpresa seemed not to care that I'd shined my girlfriend. My girlfriend? Did I think of Sharon that way? Also, was Shpresa jealous?

Sharon lowered her voice. "Billy was going to let us use his sister's room today."

"Oh." She'd been hinting around about us doing it. The other day, she'd even laughingly suggested, while I was getting my ass beat in

77

ping pong by Billy, that I buy some condoms. I figured she was joking. "Sorry."

Why did I go to Rob's? Darn it.

"I should bicycle over to your house tomorrow. Palm Aire's not that far. Maybe a mile or so." Shpresa's family lived out that way, toward McNabb Road. I thought it would be smart to meet Sharon's parents. After all, she had met mine.

"Who were you with again today at Rob's house?" She ignored my request to hang out at her house.

"A kid from my gifted class. He's a freshman at OP next year, too. Glenn Austin."

Silence bled through the line. For a second, I thought we'd been disconnected. Then she spoke. "Is he–he's not related to Dorothea Austin, is he? She's in my grade."

"Uh, I don't know." Unless they lived in my neighborhood, I didn't really know much about kids in older grades, even those who had gone to OP Middle. For instance, I might have seen Sharon once when she was in eighth grade and I was in seventh grade, but I didn't know her. "Maybe?"

"Is he a n***er? 'Cause Dorothea is."

My mouth went dry. Peter's dad used that word once around us kids, but my parents taught me it was an ugly word that I shouldn't ever say. How could such a foul word roll so easily from Sharon's beautiful lips? I pictured her on the other end of the phone, and the face I envisioned was no longer hers but that of a bizarro-world look-alike with bloodless skin, soulless black eyes, and a grim flat line for a mouth. My stomach turned. "Why would you call him that? That's..."

"Steven, you know they are what they are. My dad says..." Her voice turned into a drone, a far-away squawking as she outlined her dad's views—her views—about people. Colored people. Jews. Arabs.

Chinese people. Jimmy Carter. She moved on to talk about gas prices and petty theft. Lots of things. My mind was buzzing like somebody had thrown a toaster into my bathtub, zapping me with ten thousand volts.

You can be anything you want to be, Steven, Shpresa said to me. *Didn't you listen to your smart friend, Rob earlier? Hang up on her. Now. It's not worth another blowjob.*

The front door opened signaling my mom and dad had returned from work. Their arrival made it easier to make my decision.

"I gotta go, Sharon. I–I'll catch you later."

"Okay. See you at Annie's tomorrow."

I don't know.

You can be anything you want to be, Shpresa repeated.

My mom, a paper bag full of groceries in one arm, entered the kitchen as I hung up the phone. "Who was that?" In the family room on the other side of the counter, my dad, groaning softly, dropped onto the couch. His work shoes clunked on the carpet as he kicked them off. The acrid smell of cigarette smoke drifted over the counter as he lit up.

"Sharon. It was Sharon on the phone."

My mom smiled as she slid a box of peanut butter cookies into the cabinet. I had brought Sharon to the house last week to meet my parents, and she had worn a cross around her neck. That was all it took for my mother to take a shine to her. "She's a nice girl. Better than the other one." She meant Annie.

"Yeah. Uh, I don't know." I didn't know much about anything anymore. Also, my mom didn't know Sharon was Annie's friend.

"Oh, no." My mom adopted a fake pout. "Young love. Is it over already for you and Sharry?"

God, she was patronizing. "Sharon. I don't know." My mind swam with dark thoughts.

My mom gently closed the kitchen cabinet and faced me where I sat on the kitchen counter beside the phone. "Steven, I have hard news."

I swallowed hard. What now?

"It's Cher."

My stomach flipped. "Is she okay?"

"She's taking longer than expected. She may not come home until after Halloween."

My heart sank into my gut. "What? No."

"I know you care for Cher, but she'll come back when she's ready. They say she's not prepared to return. It's a process. We need to trust the process."

From the couch, my dad made an indecipherable sound, a loud, out-of-place 'hurh' that seemed to indicate displeasure at my mom's revelation. I wondered what he was thinking.

"We'll still go to see her. On Saturdays."

"Do I have to go again?" I loved Cher, but I didn't think I could take another moment in that hangar. I'd visited the Sprout sessions twice, each Saturday morning since she'd gone in, and it was two times too many.

My mom's eyes registered surprise. "Oh. I—your father and I will talk about it. Cher will miss you if you don't go."

"She'll understand." I struggled for the right words. "I'm not a druggie, so it makes me feel weird going there."

My mom's face hardened. "Your father and I will discuss it."

Cher won't understand why you're not there, Steven.

Screw off, Shpresa. I just...can't.

It would be over four months before I saw Cher again. Longer before I saw Sharon. I wouldn't run into Sharon again for two years. I broke up with her the next day over the phone, and I avoided Annie's house, as well as Peter and Billy, for most of the rest of the summer.

In mid-August, my parents, fraught with worry over the supposedly egregious drug use at OP High, made a rush decision to send me to a parochial school, Marianist High, about fifteen miles south of us in Hollywood. The Catholic school gave me an academic scholarship so we could afford it, and they allowed me to attend even though I wasn't Catholic. The day after Labor Day, my parents, on their way to jobs in Miami, dropped me at my new school, and they picked me up on their way home. I knew nobody at my new school; it was like starting over completely. And maybe it was okay that I was brand new there. I could be anybody I wanted to be. Then, November came, and with it, Cher. Sort of...

Stepford Cousin

Saturday, November 22, 1980

It's not her, I thought. The people at The Sprout had analyzed Cher's body and brain, fed all the data into a super-computer in their evil airplane hangar, and they'd fashioned a duplicate of her. *She's a robot with no true emotions.* I knew by the semi-vacant, glossy stare she gave me when she walked in our front door. Not a 'hey, kiddo,' with the joyful bubble in her tone, but a 'hello, Steven,' weighed down with barely submerged notes of judgment and detachment. And something else stained her dull greeting, something far underneath: Pain. There was anguish buried deep in my cousin's voice.

I stood in Cher's open bedroom doorway as she unpacked her duffel. My eyes flickered down the hall, glancing at my sister's room. Marie was at a friend's house, making herself scarce. Maybe she still felt guilty about Cher, but I didn't think so; she was only making it easy on herself by being absent. The only thing Marie held onto was vengeance, not guilt. Even if my sister hadn't gotten me back for stealing from her last summer, the look in her eyes, her alligator grin when she passed me in the hallway or in the kitchen each morning, told me she had neither forgotten nor forgiven me.

"You can come into my room, Steven." Cher waved me into her bedroom.

Careful, Steven.

I sat on Cher's bed as she patted perfectly folded shirts and pants into her dresser, fitting them in just so. She didn't speak, and the silence grew unbearable. "Uh, sorry I didn't come again to The Sprout after the first couple of times."

Her eyes, so distant, appraised me like she was a pod person from *Invasion of the Body Snatchers* eyeing up her next victim. "It's okay. Why didn't you come?"

"I don't know. It wasn't my thing."

"Wasn't your thing." She repeated my statement flatly.

I shifted on her mattress, my butt cheeks suddenly itching. "It made me uncomfortable."

"Made you uncomfortable." She closed her bedroom door. Closed me in. She sat beside me on her bed, took my hands in hers. "The front row is beautiful, Steven. Maybe you'd like to sit there. Make it your home."

I gulped. "I sat there. The two times I went."

She smiled, the corners of her mouth tugging up like a marionette master was jiggling the ends. "Not on that side. Not that front row. I meant you can sit on the other side. As a resident. As a sprout. To become a flower."

"Oh. I mean, why would I?"

"Why would you?" Her monotone made every hair on my arms stand on end. Why did she keep repeating stuff I said?

"I like—I don't do drugs."

83

I didn't do drugs, at least I hadn't done anything for many months. Before I broke up with Sharon, my friends and I got high on a joint we rolled from the pot I stole from my sister. But since then, nothing. I had no opportunity to do drugs or anything bad, really, because my parents drove me down to high school in Hollywood every day to hang out with kids I didn't know. Last week, taking my cue from Rob, who seemed fearless about wading into football, I started wrestling practice, and my parents picked me up after. I had stopped hanging out with Billy, Peter, Annie, and Joey, who had returned from New York.

Cher blinked. A sign she was human. Her voice came out a whisper, and she leaned toward me. "I made a deal with the devil for you, Steven."

"W–what?" Goose pimples shivered up my arms.

She explained in a low rasp. "I made a deal with the devil because I love you. It's beautiful at The Sprout, but Jesus came to me in a dream and told me this summer wasn't the right time for you to be there. God told me to make a deal with the devil. Rebeccah and Simon asked me and asked me about you, over and over, but I never told them. Because God didn't want me to tell them. And finally, they believed me."

What the heck was she talking about? She must have seen the confusion on my face because she stated, "I told them about Marie. I told them your sister did drugs too. I didn't tell them the marijuana they found was hers, though." She dropped her chin to the side, staring at the carpet beside her. "Your parents decided not to bring Marie into the fold. Not to make her a sprout." She paused while my front teeth nearly tore a hole in my bottom lip, biting back so many feelings—shock, resentment, anger.

They. Let. Marie. Go.

They did. They still don't know the pot they found was hers, but they believed Cher when she told them Marie did drugs with friends. And because

84

they had no proof, they let it go. Or maybe because Marie gets away with EVERYTHING.

Cher continued as if she could hear my thoughts. "That was your parents' decision to make. Your mother and father are God's stewards of their children. Our guardians. My guardians. We must obey them."

Yeah, but you're eighteen now, Cher. You're a grown-up.

She is an adult. But she doesn't feel free to make choices like an adult. Not anymore.

Please, stop talking Shpresa.

"Even so, that doesn't change what I did for you." Her voice was level. "Steven, you and I and Jesus above and Satan below know you have done drugs. When the time is right, Jesus will call you to the front row of The Sprout. But I may go to hell for you. For not telling." She wiped a tear from her eye. "Because I love God, and I love you. But it's beautiful, Steven. What I've learned. The joy in my heart, I want you to feel it, too. I know I did the right thing."

Why was she crying if she was so darned happy? Why did her voice waver when she claimed to have done the right thing? Why was she spewing a mystifying barrage of pseudo-religious babble?

"Okay. But I really don't do drugs, Cher. You know me. I don't. I go to school in Hollywood, and I don't even hang out with the neighborhood kids anymore. I started wrestling." My lip trembled. This was not my cousin. This was somebody else. A replacement. A machine. A Stepford cousin. I wiped my burning eyes, blinking back tears. "I love you, Cher."

She was always the kind one. She still is kind.

She squeezed my hand. "I heard you were wrestling at your new school. That's good. And I love you, Steven. When it's time, you'll go in." She stood and continued unpacking.

"Are you enrolling in college for next year? For January." Maybe changing the subject would help this sickness in my stomach go away.

"Maybe. I'm not sure that's God's plan for me as a flowering child of His." My fake cousin, this automaton, presented me with a close-lipped smile. "When it's time, Steven, time for you, you'll go to The Sprout."

Why did she keep saying that? I made no response. I didn't even nod. I simply got up and walked out of her room. I slunk into my bedroom, shut my door, and wept into my pillow.

Another Door Closing

Cher didn't enroll in community college for the spring semester of 1981. Four days after Christmas, on a Monday morning, I found her.

"Take the Long Way Home" by Supertramp played on Marie's phonograph in the background, down the hall and a million miles away. My cousin's thin limp arm hung over the tub, an ugly dark slit gaping on her pale wrist. Rivulets of blood ran from the gash to her fingertips, staining the yellow bathmat below with a drip, drip, drip. Her head had drifted under the crimson pool, long brown hair fanned out on its surface.

I sobbed and grabbed Cher under her arms, dragging her placid, ashy face above the warm, crimson-stained water, which sloshed onto the tiles and baptized my bare legs in her blood. I howled until Marie came running from her bedroom to witness the aftermath with widened eyes and a slack jaw. "You did this!" I shouted at my sister through my sobs. "You did this!" Marie disappeared, footsteps pounding down the hall, and several minutes later, an ambulance screamed up, flashing red lights dancing like demonic spirits outside the frosted bathroom

87

window, its siren wailing as if crying out to God who, for the moment, didn't seem to be listening.

Two men in dark blue busted into the house, dragged me away from her. Started shouting orders at each other.

But it was too late.

Our In-between - 1980 to 1982

Dissolution

1980 to 1982

Tragedy, the loss of a beautiful shining light like my cousin, Cher, can pull a family closer together and close their ranks, or it can drive a family apart. The latter proved true for us, and like every crumbling family, as I've since learned from reading Tolstoy, we broke apart in our own distinct way. For a family such as ours, already frayed around the edges and fractured in the middle, Cher's death didn't drive us apart as much as it dissolved us, slowly, like a sugar cube fizzing into a glass of water, grains swirling up and mixing with the clear liquid until nothing was left of the sweetness. We vanished from each other.

My mother, who never saw Cher's body, especially not in all its bloodied and ashen sadness, glommed onto Cher's death as an opportunity to glorify her God. She molded her own bizarre story around the edges of the pain and self-recrimination the woman would never allow herself to fully embrace. My mom built a sturdy fiction: Cher Rankin was a lovely but deeply troubled soul; God had called her to a better place; The Sprout had done what good work it could do for

Cher, but in the end, it wasn't enough. And so on. Linnea Jacobs, birth name Linnea Rankin, built a hard shell of lies around herself, a barrier no one could penetrate.

My sister grew distant, and, at least in the first few days after Cher died, when the morning light hit Marie just right, you could see a wisp of guilt flitting across her face. This secretly made me happy, both that Marie was suffering for what she'd done but also that she was human. Sometimes I wondered if my sister, with her tanned beach body, perfect blonde hair, and cold blue eyes, was an evil robot or a serial killer like Ted Bundy, devoid of real emotions.

I didn't fully embrace my feelings either, at least not at the time. The shame I felt over Cher's death—which I was keenly aware would not have happened had I not stolen Annie's pot and set in motion the wheels of ignorance—settled in my stomach like a rock. I buried this culpability there in my gut, doing my best to keep it tamped down. But sometimes, staring at the closed bedroom door in the middle of our hallway, tears would well in my eyes, and I'd turn away. In those awful moments, I'd scramble to think about something else, so my quivering legs wouldn't stumble from under me, and I wouldn't take a nosedive and curl up on the hall carpet, a blubbering fetal mess. A month after Cher died, my mom asked me if I wanted to move back to the larger bedroom that my cousin had used, my old bedroom, but I stayed inside the smallest room, my tiny closet. I couldn't even begin to think about moving into Cher's old space. A not-so-small part of me feared if I moved into Cher's former bedroom that she might haunt me like Shpresa haunted me, except this would be worse because of my guilt. Would Cher's ghost be upset? Would Shpresa's ethereal cautionary voice, which I heard more sporadically over the next two years, be replaced by Cher's more reproachful, harsh tone? An angry spirit?

The same way I interred my guilt, I likewise buried myself in my schoolwork and my athletics. When I wasn't studying or lifting weights or practicing wrestling, I slapped on Asics Tiger running shoes, and I ran outside, sculpting the young man I wanted to become. Or maybe I was running from who I really was. I ran, and I ran, and I ran—in the fall-summer, the winter-summer, the spring-summer, the sweltering, hundred-degree summer-summer. I ran out of my neighborhood, down Prospect Road to Powerline Road, up Powerline Road to McNabb Road. All the roads. I ran many, many miles. I ran far away, quelling the desire to keep running up and out of Florida, and always finding my way back home. I wanted to run far enough away to sweat out my complicity in killing my kind cousin. I ran so the heartbreak might seep through my arteries and burn inside my lungs, which gasped for absolution and wheezed for fresh air. I distracted myself with friendships, too. I became friendly with one of my high school wrestling partners, Chris Halligan. We'd spend time down in Hollywood on the weekends, eating his mother's lasagna, swimming in his pool, and hanging at the Hollywood beach. When I turned sixteen my sophomore year, in March of 1982, I spent every weekend driving my parents' car down to Hollywood. There, I met up with Chris and others, and, although I was shy, I slowly made friends with some of the girls. I dated a wrestling cheerleader, Rosie Gonzalez, borrowing my dad's car yet again to see her on the weekends.

I drifted from my neighborhood, and the neighborhood drifted from me.

I'd nod at my sister each morning before school, but other than the first few days after Cher's death when I caught the pain on Marie's face, I generally had no idea what she was thinking. No idea what Marie was doing.

My sister continued to go out most nights, growing even bolder about her on-and-off relationship with Sal Bucci. She continued to do her own thing, unimpeded, free from any consequences. Typical Marie. In a rare moment, as I passed her in our house's hallway, her icy blue eyes would flicker, and I knew she had not forgotten her promise to punish me for stealing from her. Or maybe that was my imagination. During those instances, though, Shpresa would surface to inform me that, yes, I was correct: Marie had neither forgotten nor forgiven me. She was merely biding her time. Even in the face of everything that had happened, my sister still held a grudge.

And my father? My father pulled the worst disappearing act of all. My father, in contrast to my mother's ability to drench herself in fantasy, was the one who identified Cher in the morgue. From the look on his face when he got back from that gruesome task, coupled with the grim portrait he presented at her funeral, it was obvious he knew a terrible travesty had occurred in our house. He didn't have a talent for fooling himself like my mother did. When Cher was alive, I could sense by the lightness with which my father spoke to Cher that he possessed a special fondness for his niece. Maybe because of Cher's kind nature, she was the daughter he'd wished he'd had, as opposed to Marie, who was a hard woman like my mother.

Over the next year or so, my father's mouth disappeared from his face. Before Cher's death, he had been growing quieter each day, almost like he had somehow acceded to my mother's belief that Cher, if she had lived, needed further rehabilitation. When Cher had gone into The Sprout, it felt like each morning my mother had sat on the edge of their bed and sewed my father's lips shut for him. With Cher's death, those sutures remained, and the skin grew over his mouth, holding his thoughts and feelings captive. I can hardly remember him uttering more than a couple of words to me or my mother here and there. It reminded me of a phrase he would say to me when I was a little boy: "Steven, a man has to keep the plates of his life spinning." Perhaps he was muttering a random word or two as a bare minimum to keep his own engine running.

I never forgot the loud 'hurh,' a simple nonsensical grunt that my dad made in July of 1980 when my mom told me Cher would be staying at The Sprout longer than anticipated. My father had communicated so much with that single utterance. His displeasure. His small rebellion. But now, for him, there was no rebelling, only strangled acceptance.

In tandem with his vow of silence, my father left his job about a year after Cher died. I'd find him sleeping on the couch when my mother brought me home from school. On the positive side, because he was listless, he stopped screaming at me and hitting me on the top of my head for minor infractions the way he had done when I was in middle school. At first, I figured he left me alone because I was getting older; I was bigger, stronger, and a better wrestler. I was more physically dangerous. In the end, I decided it was because he had grown tired. Very, very tired.

In the summer of 1982, my father found another job as a marketer for a cruise line in Miami. So, he once again sat in the Grand Prix on weekday mornings, this time as a passenger, when my mom drove me to school and him to work. But despite his new job, he remained quiet in the car and in our house. I suspected that deep down he harbored many private thoughts, but I never imagined he was keeping the great secret I discovered almost two years after my cousin's suicide.

So, life went on. Or should I say, life stumbled, trudged, crawled, sprinted, fizzled, and sputtered on. I suppose The Sprout went on, too, run by Howel Carnavale, whom I'd never met, and his acolytes, Simon and Rebeccah, doing their twisted thing out beside the Everglades. But I had no idea at the time what was going on there. Then, in late June of

1982, Marie, who had turned eighteen in May, graduated high school, and she told my family how she really felt. And it was as if my sister, in airing her grievances, gave an enormous gear a monstrous shove. Everything started all over again.

1982

Dog Days

Fantasmas

Friday, June 11, 1982

The mustard cord stretched taut from the phone base on our kitchen wall. It wrapped around the corner and ended in the nook between the hallway and the family room, where I sat with the handset to my face, back against the wall, knees to my chest. Marie strode down the hallway, but I kept my eyes on my own bare knees. Like an apparition in my peripheral vision, she glided to my right and into the kitchen. For a moment, I worried that she might press her finger on the plunger on the phone in the kitchen and disconnect my call, but that feeling passed. Marie wasn't small in her actions, and I knew she wouldn't do something that trivial. When my sister was ready to bother me, more specifically to wreak vengeance, I would know it.

"You there, Steven? Thought I lost you." Rosie's voice pulled me from my thoughts.

"Uh, yeah. So, tonight?"

"I need to ask my parents about tonight. Why not tomorrow night? A bunch of us are going to the beach tomorrow. We could go out after."

"My sister's graduating high school tomorrow. My dad made reservations at this restaurant down on the intercoastal. It's only my family." I said this with a tinge of guilt; I wanted to bring Rosie to our dinner, but Marie wasn't dating anybody, not that we knew, and my parents had made it clear the celebration was only for us four.

"Okay. Hold on, Steven. Here's my mom, let me ask her."

Silence ruled the line. Rosie must have covered the phone with her hand.

"Hey." She came back on the line. "She wants to know what we're going to see."

"A new movie by Steven Spielberg. *Poltergeist*. It's playing at the theater on Sheridan. Then we'll hit Swensen's Ice Cream." Swensen's was code for the Hollywood Beach Hotel.

"Mamá, vamos a ver *Poltergeist*. Por Steven Spielberg."

"¿Esa es una pelicula del diablo?" her mother asked in the background.

I'd learned enough Spanish in two years to know that her mother had asked a problematic question; she wanted to know if the film was about the devil. "No, no es el diablo," I said hurriedly. "Tell her it's about ghosts. Like Casper." Well, not like Casper...but, anyway.

"No se trata del diablo. Sólo tiene fantasmas. Como, eh, Casper."

I couldn't believe she used the Casper thing. I was half joking about that. Her mother was speaking now, but farther away from the phone and in rapid Spanish, which I couldn't decipher.

Rosie whispered into the phone. "She's crossing herself. Oh, boy. Now she's saying there's no such thing as aliens, that we are the only one of God's creatures made in his image. I think she's talking about *Close Encounters*." Rosie chuckled dryly. "Dios mío," she murmured. "All this, over a movie."

101

Close Encounters? How had her mom transitioned from *Poltergeist* to *Close Encounters of the Third Kind*? I guessed because they were both Spielberg movies.

"Fantasmas, Mamá! Solo fantasmas! Hold up, Steven."

Silence struck our conversation again for a very long minute as, I presumed, Rosie placed her hand over the receiver and hashed things out with her mother.

"Okay, I'm back. It's a good thing she likes you. She's not happy you're asking me out the same day, though. She told me to tell you that. What time should I be ready?"

"Uh, there's an eight-thirty show. I'll pick you up at seven-thirty. Like in three hours."

"Always early, Steven. Okay. Bye. See you then." Her last words came out breathy—so light and carefree. It's one of the reasons I liked Rosie, her lightness.

"Bye." I waited for the click on the line, and I rose from the floor and walked the handset into the kitchen, where my mother stood, not making a show of doing anything other than eavesdropping on my conversation. My sister had somehow disappeared, although I didn't remember seeing her walk back down the hallway toward her bedroom. Maybe she'd drifted through the laundry room and out of the garage.

Ghosts. Fantasmas.

My mother subconsciously touched her cross. "You're learning Spanish now."

"I've been learning Spanish for two years at school. Rosie's mother speaks more Spanish than English when she's home."

"When are you going to introduce us to Rosalie?"

"Rosie." What was this thing with my mom getting my girlfriends' names wrong? As far as her meeting Rosie, maybe never. It was my mom's own fault for shipping me down to a Catholic school in

Hollywood. It was inconvenient to drive my girlfriend back up here to Fort Lauderdale just so my parents could meet her. "I don't know when you'll meet her. You saw her at wrestling matches this year." Wasn't that enough?

"I know, yes, Rosie. The cute little dark Mexican one. But you started going out after the season, so we never got to say hello."

Little dark Mexican one? Jesus Christ, Rosie's a person. I made a mental note: Do not introduce my mother to Rosie's parents if they ever come to a wrestling match.

"She could drive up here to Oakland Park."

I rummaged in the fridge, grabbed a bottle of Sunny Delight, and shook it. It was almost empty, and I swigged the dregs of the juice from the bottle. "She's not sixteen until August. So, she can't drive anywhere on her own yet."

The corners of my mother's mouth drooped. "What have I told you about drinking out of the container?"

I shook the bottle. "It's empty." I tossed it into the trash can under the sink.

"What was that I heard about diablo? You're not seeing a devil movie like *The Exorcist*, are you?"

Jeez, different cultures, same mother problem. "No, it's a ghost story. A poltergeist is a ghost. It haunts the house. Because the spirit is unhappy. Something bad happened to it in life. Or something like that."

Or something like that.

A shiver ran up my spine as I realized what Shpresa meant. As I realized what I was saying.

My mother and I entered an old, silent movie, our eyes locked in a black and white world, connecting in the stark knowledge that our house, in one way or another, was haunted. A single word played in my mind the way I'm certain it played in hers: Cher.

Fantasma.

So much blood in the bathroom. Sometimes I'd wake with a start in the middle of the night. Drenched in sweat, not blood. Wheezing. Afraid. Frightened of something lying, invisible and insidious, right beside me in my bed. Or on my bare chest.

"Linnea, would you give the kid a goddamned break, and let him go?" It was my father. His muffled, disembodied voice floated from the family room couch pressed against the waist-high wall on the other side of the kitchen counter. My mother and I swung our heads in his direction. That sentence contained more words than I could remember him saying in the last month, and it broke us from our mesmerized state. A column of smoke twisted up from where he reclined smoking his Kent cigarettes.

Fantasmas.

I wondered, could it have been something else, somebody else, who prompted my father to speak on my behalf? Could Cher's spirit have interfered in my favor? And why would she do a thing like that when I was responsible for her becoming suicidal, for dying so young? It was an odd day when a guilty thought like this didn't rattle inside my head. But maybe Cher was on my side now. Maybe?

No, Steven. It's only the ebb and flow of your dad's depression. It's got nothing to do with Cher.

Is my father depressed?

I think so, yes. And someday, you're going to need to cleanse yourself of this recrimination. You need to get to a place where it's an atypical day in which you think about Cher, versus the other way around.

I don't know how.

I know you don't. But you'll figure it out, one way or the other. Oh, here's your mom.

My mom had snapped her fingers in front of my face. "Where did you go?"

"Just thinking. So, can I have the car keys…please?"

"They're in the ashtray in the foyer hall, same as always." My dad's immaterial voice came at us from beyond.

My mom gave me a curt nod to let me know she consented. "Have fun. Don't get home too late. It's your sister's big day tomorrow."

"I have to take a shower first." *I need to scrub out the dirt. Scrub myself harder. Get the stain out.*

Someday, Steven, you'll need to be kinder to yourself.

Yeah, well, not today, Shpresa. And don't show up when Rosie and I park at the Hollywood Beach Hotel after the movie, either. It was weird last time you did it.

Be kind. Be generous. Don't ask for more than she is willing to give. Be a gentleman, Steven. Shpresa rattled off the admonishments one or both of my parents should have told me about how to behave when things got hot and heavy in the car's back seat.

I'm always a gentleman, right?

I locked the bathroom door, stripped, started the shower, and waited for the water to warm. I stepped in, soaping myself and thinking about Rosie…to take the edge off. When I finished, Shpresa spoke: *There. Feel better now? You are a gentleman, Steven. I suppose that's not one of the things I need to warn you about.*

What things do you need to warn me about?

I knew that answer. I knew because I didn't always listen. Like stealing a bag of pot.

Shpresa failed to respond to my question, though. She was gone for now.

My date went fine. The movie was great, and Rosie and I had a good time afterward. No intercourse, as usual. Because Catholicism. But of course, parked in a dark corner of the near-vacant Hollywood Beach Hotel lot, there were things kids did, things Rosie and I did, to momentarily unburden our sexual cravings while skirting the baby-making process. The things we did in the backseat never bothered me afterward, but Rosie admitted to me that she confessed our 'sins' to her priest. She promised me that she kept her confessions vague, providing no real details. Even so, it was a little weird to imagine her telling her priest about our sex life. Also, her priest could have been one of my high school teachers. So that was strange, too, wondering if my English teacher, whom we affectionately called Father Forehead, knew what she and I had done in the back seat of my car.

I spent part of the next day—late morning and early afternoon on Saturday—at Rob's, hanging with him and Glenn. Rob's dad had sent his Apple III computer back because it didn't work well. His father owned a different type of computer, now, one that looked like the computer from gifted class in eighth grade, but he wouldn't let us go near it. I asked Rob what his dad did, and he told me his dad did something with the government, but he wasn't sure what. Rob had the nicest home on our block, a massive corner house with real tile on the floors; back in 1972, it had been the model they'd shown to attract people to buy the houses when the neighborhood was built. The family room was almost all windows, and, of course, there was the pool. It was pleasant, and I liked hanging out there. It didn't seem to matter that the three of us went to different high schools—Rob to his magnet school in Delray, Glenn to OP High, and me to a Catholic school in Hollywood— when we got together, we meshed easily, talking about books and computers and girls. Rob was dating somebody from his school, and Glenn said he had a girlfriend in his neighborhood, which my mom called the ghetto. Something about the way Glenn spoke of his girlfriend, giving no details and struggling to answer questions about her, made me wonder if he was lying about her, but I didn't care whether she was real or not.

I came home that afternoon from Rob's house feeling good. I took a shower, dressed in slacks and a short-sleeved button-down shirt like my mother had instructed, and accompanied my parents to Marie's graduation from OP High, held in their big gymnasium.

Her graduation was boring. The interesting stuff came later. Marie went somewhere with friends after the ceremony, and she said she'd meet us back at the house at six. My mother, sitting at the kitchen table, was tapping her foot by the time Marie waltzed in the door a half-hour late, still wearing her gown, cap in her hand. My sister brought a sharp edge into the house with her, a buzz that vibrated my bones. Her light blue irises were almost fully blotted out by her black pupils, which were about as dilated as dilated could be. Years later in 1988, when I became a bartender between college and graduate school, I'd do cocaine for the first time, tasting the bitter numbness on my tongue, and I'd retroactively remember Marie as having been high on coke. If my mother knew Marie was flying high on something, she didn't get a chance to react because my sister stalked into the house and went on the attack almost immediately. First, she flipped her black mortar cap at us like a frisbee. It landed perfectly in the middle of our round kitchen table where my mom, dad, and I sat. The green and black tassel fanned out on the hardwood surface.

My mom's eyebrows poked up. "Are you ready to—"

Marie punched her waist with her own fists. The pose reminded me of a petulant toddler "I'm not going out with you tonight."

"What?" My mother's tone was hard.

My father tapped his cigarette ash into a small tray on the kitchen table, and with a flat, unchanging expression, he stared at Marie through his gold-rimmed glasses. I expected him to say something, but he didn't.

"I said, I'm not going to dinner with you. I'm going out with my boyfriend, Rick Stumpf."

Aah, surfer dude, Rick Stumpf. Last summer I'd worked at Wendy's, and as I'd taken out a bag of trash, Rick had zipped through the drive-through in a sparkly green convertible Corvette, a surfboard somehow strapped to its back. A gorgeous, tanned, bikini-clad girl with straight blonde hair and dark sunglasses, sat beside him. The girl had frozen me with her sunglasses, her face twisted into a sneer like I was a bag of garbage. It was humiliating, but some of us had to work. Rick, always shirtless with a perfectly bronzed surfer body and sun-bleached blond hair, only dated the most attractive girls. I supposed Marie qualified.

"Who is Rick Stumpf?"

"He surfs," I muttered.

"Shut up, Steven," Marie snapped. "Nobody asked you."

"I was just saying." I crossed my arms.

My mother stood. "Marie, this is your graduation dinner. Your father has been looking forward to this for weeks."

Had he? It didn't seem to me that my father looked forward to much of anything anymore.

Marie got face to face with my mom, invading her space. For the first time in my life, I wondered if she and my mom, who usually traded barbs on the boundaries of direct confrontation, were going to get into a physical fight. They were about the same size, maybe a few inches shorter than me, but they were tall for women, about five seven, maybe taller. It would be like a couple of Amazonian women fighting.

If they fight, my money is on your mom.

Me too, Shpresa. But that's not how Marie does things.

I literally saw the spittle land on my mother's cheek when Marie, bristling, jabbed at my mom with her next words: "I'm not coming to anything with you anymore. And I'm going to tell you a few more things."

Dios mío.

My mom swallowed hard. Was she cracking? She clutched at her cross.

"I'm leaving this house. Tonight. I'm moving in with Rick. I'm eighteen, and I'll do what I want. I can't spend another minute in this place with you."

"Marie." My father uttered her name weakly, begging for mercy.

"This is absurd," my mother replied. "Marie you—"

"And guess what? I do drugs. How about that? I've always done drugs. But I never keep them here. You can't call the police. There's no grass, no bennies, and no coke in the house. You know what cocaine is, Mother? You won't find it. Call the cops. You've got nothing on me. I won't go to The Sprout. I'd go to prison first."

My mother's body vibrated slightly, like a cold-induced shiver, but she didn't speak.

"Marie, we know you're kidding." My father stubbed out his cigarette, his voice still pleading with my sister for her absolution.

"And you know what else? That pot you found two years ago, the pot Cher said was hers. That pot was mine."

My throat tightened, and my palms started to sweat. This was it. My sister was going to give me up. I was going into that awful place. But Marie didn't even glance at me; she kept her eyes on my mom's.

My mother sighed. "Marie, we all know it was Cher's marijuana. You don't have to...if you think this will somehow lift her memory up...please, don't lie."

My father remained quiet.

"We all killed her." My sister sighed. "You killed her, too, Mother. Except you're so wrapped up in your own garbage that you'll never see it. It's why I can't stand you. It's why Daddy can't stand you."

That's when it happened.

Marie's eyes made a tiny shift toward my father. He raised his hound dog eyes from his next cigarette to meet hers. Through the thick lenses of his glasses, I recognized his tacit acknowledgment that he believed Marie was telling the truth and that the pot was hers. He knew. And Marie knew he knew. And now I knew he knew. Everyone but my mom knew. My father just as quickly dropped his eyes back to the dirty tray filled with ashes and cigarette stubs.

He knew it was Marie. Or he suspected. He figured those drugs weren't Cher's. Maybe he knew they were yours, too, Steven. But he let Cher go inside. Instead of Marie.

No wonder he's been so sad. Maybe he knew why Cher took the fall. Maybe he knew about the abortion, too.

How much did he know?

I'd never heard Shpresa ask a pointed question like this. Again, not for the first time, I wondered if Shpresa was me talking to myself in my head.

"Are you gonna call the cops, Mother? Try to send me to The Sprout because I do drugs now and then?"

"Get out of my house." My mother's mouth had flattened. "Get out, you druggie. You are not welcome here." Her face reddened, and she maintained a religious grip on her tiny cross. Her eyes watered. Marie had broken her, but the cross, and whatever story it helped her concoct, would paste together her jagged pieces.

Marie chuckled dryly. "I'll get Rick to come by and grab the rest of my things tomorrow." My sister turned to me, and she cupped the side of my face with one cool hand. How could her skin be so cool? It was one hundred degrees out, we kept our air conditioning at seventy-nine degrees, and she was wearing a black graduation gown over her dress. "I haven't forgotten you, Steven. We're not finished yet, little bro. You be good." She smiled, a criminal smile.

Marie spun away from us. Just as quickly, she turned back. "Bye, Daddy." Those two words screamed that she wanted to run to him and give him one last hug. Plant a kiss on his stubbly cheek. A pat on his back. But she wasn't going to give my mother the satisfaction.

"Marie," he called mournfully as she vanished into the bowels of our house on a mission to gather some of her crap—presumably, her drugs and maybe some clothes, makeup, and a hair dryer.

"Let her go." My mother slipped a cigarette from my father's pack and lit up, only the second time I'd seen her smoke. She breathed in sharply as if she wanted to saturate her lungs with the gray cloud. I wondered if she smoked when I wasn't around. We didn't keep alcohol in our house except for a very old bottle of Cutty Sark scotch. Did my mom drink? What else didn't I know about her? My mom sat beside my dad at the kitchen table.

My dad removed his glasses. He wiped at both eyes.

Was he crying?

"We'll go to dinner without her." My mother blew a stream of smoke across the table, the gray cloud dissipating between my father and me. My dad, his mouth sewn shut, skin stretched smooth over his lips, rose, walked into the family room, and plopped onto his couch with a soft sigh.

We didn't go to dinner that night.

And Marie never came back to live with us.

Marie returned to the house sometimes, though. I'd encounter her marching through the halls when my parents weren't home or hear her rummaging around in her bedroom, which my dad told my mom to leave as it was in the event she came back. When I saw her, she would give me a nod and flatly say, 'Steven,' but she never spoke to me otherwise. It made me wonder if she was stashing drugs in our home and using it as a safe space. But I never looked in her room. I knew if I did, it would lead to bad things.

Why? A reminder of how all this started: In the first semester of eighth grade, I was infatuated with a girl named Carrie Sullivan. Carrie was tanned and pretty, with straight dark hair that fell to her shoulders. She and I were partners in woodshop, and one day we talked about weed. She was wearing these tight white jeans that day. So tight, and I was thirteen and not above stealing a glance at the curves of Carrie's butt. That night, I searched my sister's room, found her stash, and stole enough to roll a thin joint. I brought it to school in my book bag and showed it to Carrie the next day, but she gave me some excuse for why she couldn't hang and smoke it together after school in the rock pit. I think Thanksgiving was coming, and she had to shop with her mom or something. Or, at least, that's what she said. Instead, I smoked the joint with Peter later. Then, months later, when Peter and I stole part of Annie's stash and I went to my sister for help hiding it, I let it slip that I knew where Marie kept her drugs. Because of that slip, my sister moved her stash. And because she moved her stash, my father found her drugs. And because of that—and other things—Cher went to The Sprout. And The Sprout killed Cher. I'd only spoken to Rebeccah one time, but in my heart, I was certain that young woman, she of the razor-sharp questions, had done the following to my cousin: torn Cher apart, ripped out her innards, replaced them with cotton fluff, sewed her back up, and sent her back to us as a scarecrow of herself. I wasn't going to make that same mistake again, nosing where I didn't belong, so I left well enough alone, left my sister alone. She had promised to take her revenge on me, and some days that possibility worried me, but most days I forgot about it.

I spent that summer alternately hanging with Rob and Glenn, my wrestling buddy Chris, and Rosie. Ultimately, I said something dumb to Rosie, and she and I broke up in late July. I hardly saw the other guys from the neighborhood at all, except one time when I passed Peter on the street, and he cursed at me for not hanging out with them anymore, asked me if I thought I was too good for them. I didn't respond, just stared at him, which seemed to infuriate him even more, making him curse at me again.

I didn't think about Annie at all. She simply dropped out of my life like Peter, Billy, and Joey. I assumed they were hanging out with her, though. Then, a chance encounter on our way to *Fast Times* led me somewhere I didn't expect to go. Back to the beginning.

Movie City 11

Saturday, August 14, 1982

The three of us stood at the edge of the open arcade, where its bright red-and-blue striped carpet met the tiled floor of the mall. At a right angle to the doorless gallery, the movie theatre's high-ceilinged entrance gaped, the ticket-sales counter a single bottom tooth in the middle of the theatre's wide mouth. The lobby beyond the theatre entrance stretched back, a massive tunnel, with a concession stand running up its middle like a narrow tongue. Past the concession stand, the broad path turned right toward the row of eleven theatres. The guts of the cinema.

Rob and I were casting glances at the ticket taker, Dave Wonka, as we argued with Glenn. "Y'all don't understand. It's not the same for me as you. It's different," Glenn pleaded with us.

Rob was insistent we do the thing, though. "Dude, Dave Wonka's right there. He's looking at me now, waiting for us. It's easy. There are so many people in line, nobody will even notice. We go in separately, like five or six people between each of us. You make believe you're handing him a ticket, but you hand him nothing. Just go through the motions and walk in. The owner isn't watching. Nobody's watching. It's foolproof. Nobody's going to get caught."

Glenn shook his head. "If you get caught, they slap your wrist, call your parents. I get caught, the fuzz beats me up out back, *and* they put me in jail. And I won't make it in jail. Y'all do it without me. I got the money to pay." After saying this, Glenn marched to the ticket booth and bought a ticket from the girl sitting there. He strode back to us and held up his ticket. "Ready for *Fast Times*."

"How did you buy a ticket to *Fast Times*?" Rob asked.

"I asked for it. What do you care? Y'all aren't even gonna have tickets to show if we get caught in the theatre."

"Good point," I admitted.

"I'll see you in there." Glenn stepped into the ticket-taking line. We watched him hand his ticket to Dave Wonka, who ripped it, handed him half, and cocked his head at Rob and me, like what's up with your buddy?

Rob sighed and walked up to the ticket booth. "Two tickets for *Fast Times at Ridgemont High*," he said loudly like he wanted to get caught. The girl shot him a dark look, but she took his cash and gave him the tickets to the rated-R movie. Rob returned and handed me one of the tickets. "You can buy the food."

"That's a raw deal. Candy, popcorn, and soda's gonna cost way more than the tickets." Glenn was already deep in the lobby and buying his own candy up at the concession stand. We entered the line, Rob in front of me.

A tap, tap on my shoulder swung me around.

It was Sharon, older and prettier, wearing light blue shorts and a white blouse, her thick, dark hair teased up in the front and clipped back by white barrettes. She looked good.

She's probably still as racist as ever.

I know, Shpresa.

"Hey."

"Uh, hey."

She was holding hands with Peter, who was doing his best to direct his attention somewhere else and look cool. Finally, his eyes drifted my way. "'Sup?"

"Not much," I answered, a knot of tension twisting in my stomach. Billy stood behind Peter, holding hands with a blonde-haired girl in a sundress. If I didn't know better, I'd say she was the same attractive girl I'd seen in my sister's boyfriend Rick Stumpf's Corvette a year ago when I was taking out the garbage at Wendy's. Or her younger sister. Billy's date didn't have sunglasses on, so it was hard to tell.

The girl looked at me blankly, and Billy gave me a nod. "'Sup, dickhead?" he said to me without a touch of irony.

I chuckled, despite myself. "Screw you, man."

I meant it as a joke, but Billy dropped his girlfriend's hand, balled his fists, and puffed his chest. "We can scrap here if you want to go, bitch." He stretched his head side to side, his slender neck cracking. The couple behind him in line took a step back.

Get him to the ground and use your wrestling skills. He's a ferret—too quick for you. He'll box you to death if you stay up on your feet.

Shpresa, since when did you become my boxing coach? I don't want to fight him at all.

"What's going on?" Rob had turned around. "Oh, hey there."

"Hey, Rob." Sharon greeted him as if Billy and I weren't about to get into a fistfight.

"Hey, Sharon. Guys. What's up?" Rob nodded at Peter and Billy, ignorant of the latter boy's clenched fists. His oblivious greeting dimmed the fire in Billy's eyes, though, and I exhaled. I hadn't even realized I'd been holding my breath.

"I was kidding, man. Sorry. It's cool," I said to placate Billy, and I returned my attention to Sharon. "How've you been?"

"Good." Her voice was clipped. But if she didn't want to talk, then why had she tapped my shoulder? Did she want to show me she was dating Peter now?

"Sharon and I go to the same school now. St. Francis," Peter piped up, his hand still gripping hers.

St. Francis, my school's crosstown rival.

"You're Catholic?" I asked her. Not that you needed to be Catholic to go to Catholic school. I was Exhibit-A for that. I was going to a Catholic school because my parents feared the evil stream of drugs that they imagined flowed like a mighty river through OP High. As if my private school had no drugs in it.

"I'm Irish Catholic, yeah," she answered.

I did not know that. Seeing them all together made me think of the old days. And Annie. "You still hang out with Annie LeFevre?" I asked her. Sharon hesitated, her mouth hanging open like she wanted to say something but was unsure of herself.

"Annie? That loser?" Peter exclaimed. "If we wanted to get buttfucked in the backwoods, maybe. We haven't hung out with that redneck in over a year."

Sharon blinked. The look on her face suggested the mention of Annie upset her, and I guessed there was more to the story than that they had simply drifted apart as friends.

Rob and I handed Dave Wonka our tickets. "Whatever," Dave mumbled to Rob, seemingly annoyed that he couldn't let us in for free. As we passed into the theatre lobby, I wondered if Dave was grabbing fake tickets from Sharon, Peter, Billy, and the nameless blonde-haired girl behind us.

Glenn waited for us near the concession counter, and we walked up to him, my former friends chattering behind us. The line at the counter had dissipated, and Rob stepped up to survey the candy. "Hey," I said to Glenn, who was tossing back a hand full of Sno-Caps. I spun to face Sharon. "Sharon, this is our friend, Glenn. Glenn this is an old friend, Sharon. And Peter and Billy."

"I've seen you riding through the neighborhood with Robbie," Peter said to Glenn. And that's all he said. If Peter ever caught Glenn riding his bike through our neighborhood without Rob or me there, I wondered what would happen. Probably nothing good.

Sharon wrinkled her nose and gave Glenn a quick, "Hey." She leaned into Peter and whispered in his ear, and they laughed.

Rob nudged me. "I ordered already, Steven. The guy's waiting for you to order."

I turned my back to Sharon so I could order. My introduction of Glenn would be the last thing I ever said to her.

After we bought our candy, popcorn, and sodas, we merged with a bunch of people streaming into the second theatre on the left to see *Fast Times*. As we entered, Glenn whispered to me, "Yo, that was some bullshit you pulled with that girl. Don't do that to me again."

I jerked my head back. Glenn, mild-mannered to a fault, never cursed. "What?"

"Is that girl your ex? You mentioned her a long time back. Sharon."

"Uh, yeah. I mean, sort of."

"She obviously doesn't like colored folk. You introduced me just to get under her skin. You used me, man."

I didn't say anything.

"Right?" he asked as we grabbed our seats, me on the end of the aisle.

"Yeah, I guess I did. Sorry I did that. But she pisses me off." I said this as Sharon and them passed us on the stairs, but she didn't glance our way.

"I get a hard enough time in the hood for digging science fiction books and computers. I get a ton of grief for being an honors student. You're my friend, Steven. Act like my friend and don't play me like that. If a bitch is racist, leave it alone. Ya' get me?"

"Yeah. Okay, man. I'm sorry. I get it." I was apologizing a lot that night.

"It's okay. Movie's starting. Let's forget about it."

Rob, who'd plopped himself two seats away from me, leaned over toward us. "Shh."

A trailer for a movie called *First Blood* with Sylvester Stallone started to play. The actor from *Rocky* ran around the woods. Woods. Backwoods. Annie. The others had stopped hanging out with Annie. Even Sharon had stopped seeing her.

What was going on with Annie LeFevre?

I forgot about Annie as the movie played because *Fast Times at Ridgemont High* was so entertaining. It was maybe the best, funniest movie I'd ever seen. Afterward, Rob, Glenn, and I imitated the funnier lines from the film as I drove Glenn back home, south of Oakland Park Boulevard, over the railroad tracks. My father's Grand Prix rolled to a stop in front of Glenn's apartment building. Cracks ran up the brick walls, and tufts of grass poked from the dirt out front.

"Get going," Glenn instructed brusquely as he shut the front passenger car door, speaking to me through the open window. "Don't hang here. See y'all later this week."

We waved goodbye to him as he disappeared around the corner.

"Not everybody gets to be everything they want to be," Rob stated, his droopy eyes lingering on Glenn's apartment building.

"Okay, Yoda," I mumbled, shifting my car into gear.

We didn't hang much with Glenn after that night. I don't remember why, but I don't think there was anything purposeful about it. I believe it mainly had to do with school starting again. I hung out with Rob less, too. Once school began, we got busy studying for tests, thinking about college, and taking harder math classes. Rob and I spent time training for our respective sports at our different high schools. Glenn played in OP High's marching band, wielding a trumpet the school loaned him. Each of us was caught in our own busy little worlds, and we drifted apart.

And there was another thing that kept me occupied for about three weeks before the start of school. I woke up the next morning thinking about our old friend, Annie LeFevre. I couldn't get Annie off my mind. So, I did something about it.

"Take It on the Run"

Monday, August 16, 1982

Maybe it was the terrible connection in my mind that linked Annie, Cher, and The Sprout, but I felt compelled to see what my old friend was doing. It was an itch in the back of my brain that needed to be scratched. After church the next day, late morning, I told my mom I was heading to Rob's. My friend's house was four houses down from mine, and I wouldn't have been able to explain why I needed the car or my bicycle to go there, so I walked down the sidewalk. I strolled past Rob's house, around the corner, and down the straight, quarter-mile street toward the front of the neighborhood. Where a grassy median lined with palms split the street, I headed left toward the field. I turned down Annie's block, the row of tiny houses on my right. On my left, the knee-high field grass was motionless in the breezeless day.

Annie's grandmother's house looked the same as it ever had, except a light brown, beat-up Pinto sat out front in place of the Impala. Dark rust, like burnt chalk, trimmed the car's wheel wells. The garage door was closed, the brown painted wood, chipped. The grass out front was patchy, and weeds sprung from between the cracks in the cement walkway that curved from the driveway to the low front stoop. On the stoop, I raised my fist to knock and hesitated.

What are you waiting for?

I don't know. I really don't even know why I'm here.

You do.

I rapped at the door. Nobody came. I rapped louder, and I heard somebody say something from behind the door. The eyehole flickered as if an eyeball had looked at me from the other side. A moment later, Annie opened the door. She looked pretty much the same as the last time I saw her before I broke up with Sharon. Her dirty-blonde hair was longer, past her shoulders, and it was clipped back. She wore a light blue tank top and high-cut dark blue athletic shorts. She had no shoes on, and light pink polish was flaking off her toenails. "Stevie." She sounded surprised to see me as she hugged the door tightly to the side of her face, only opening it a crack as if she was hiding something or trying to keep an animal from bounding out of the house. "What are you doin' here?"

"I saw Sharon. We were at the movies."

"Uh, yeah, that's nice. What'd that bitch say?"

"Nothing. I thought of you. I, uh, was wondering how you were doing."

Her hard expression softened, and she glanced at the driveway. "You came by yourself? None of your buddies?"

"I don't hang out with them anymore." A shadow passed over her face, and her eyes darted about as if she was trying to decide something. "Can I come in?"

She sighed. "Okay."

The inside of her house smacked me in the face. "Whoa. What happened to all your stuff?" Virtually all the furniture had vanished from the living room and from the kitchen, too. In the middle of the room sat a giant wooden spool, the kind that would hold cable; it sat on one round end, and on the exposed circular end were an ashtray, a textbook, and a glass filled with a brown drink, maybe soda or iced tea. Two folding lawn chairs in front of the makeshift table completed the sparse setup.

She sat in one of the chairs and took a drag from a cigarette that had been resting in the ashtray. "I had to sell the furniture to a friend. I needed quick money earlier this year. What's the matter, you don't like cigarette smoke, now?"

"What?"

"You wrinkled your nose. Like my smoke's making you sick."

"I–my wrestling coach tells us to stay away from cigarette smoke. That it's bad for our physical conditioning."

She inspected me, her eyes stopping on my arms. "You do look jacked. You filled out some, Stevie. Cigarette smoke can't hurt you by just sitting near it."

I shrugged, and she stubbed out the cigarette. "There."

I craned my neck toward the kitchen and the sunroom in the back, also devoid of furniture. "Your, uh, grandma?" I knew the answer.

"She died," she stated plainly.

"Oh. Sorry."

"Thanks."

"I know you took care of her."

She squinted at me. "You don't know the first thing about me, do you? We was friends how many years? First time y'all came down here, I was maybe ten or eleven. But I lived here for a bunch of years before that with my grandma. *She* was supposed to take care of *me*."

I didn't know how to count the years of our friendship. It seemed so random that we would visit Annie's house. And I didn't know what to say about her grandmother. My mother would say, 'well she's with God,' but somehow that didn't seem right to say. So, I kept quiet. "I came from Tennessee," she stated.

"Did you? Did you come right from there to live with your grandmother?" I knew she had told Peter and Billy something about her mother doing drugs.

"I's with my mama up there. She was doin' stuff she wasn't supposed to be." She paused. "Heroin. Smack."

"Oh."

"She moved us down here to Fort Lauderdale. We moved in with Grandma, and I slept on the couch. I was little so it was okay. Then Mama left. I might have been…I think I was six. So, 1970, maybe. They couldn't find my mama. Who knows, maybe she died. My grandma became my guardian."

I was nodding. Part of me was glad she was telling me this. I felt, somehow, honored that she would share her story with me. "But then you became her guardian when she got sick."

She laughed. "Stevie, a kid can't be an adult's guardian. She got sick slow. But lucky for me, she always knew who I was. I didn't take her to a doctor. I couldn't. The social workers woulda come and took me away if they thought she couldn't take care of me. So, she had money in her bank account, and I'd forge checks to withdraw enough money to feed us. I'd deposit her Social Security checks. This house was hers. My grandpa left her money for that before he died. But she stopped paying bills, and I had to write checks for electric and water and property taxes. For like three or four years.

Annie was doing grown-up stuff all that time. "That sounds hard."

"It wasn't really."

"That's why you dropped out of school."

"I dropped out of school because my grandma started to wander. I'd lock the doors, but she'd find a way out. One time, I found her walking all the way up by your cul-de-sac. I had to be in the house with her as much as possible. It seemed like smoking a little grass slowed her down, stopped her wandering, so I'd give it to her when I needed to shop or go to the bank."

I sighed, scanned the empty house, stopping on Annie's forlorn eyes and then gazing at the white popcorned ceiling. "It sounds…lonely," I said, looking back at her for confirmation.

Her head seemed to vibrate, and she gave me an inscrutable look. "Mmm," was all she said.

"So, what happened?"

"She got out."

"Oh. Out where?"

"She got out of the house one night and took her car. She crashed it in a gully." She blinked, her eyes becoming watery. "Dumb old lady drowned herself in a canal."

My bottom lip trembled, and I sucked it in. I reached over and touched her arm. "I'm so sorry."

She turned her face away from me. When she turned back, fresh tears glistened on her cheeks, and she wiped them away with her fingertips. "Thanks."

"So, what happened?"

"It was a week before my birthday when she died. They was gonna put me in a home, but I ran away for a week. I turned myself in on St. Patrick's Day, and there was nothing they could do. My grandma had a will, and I inherited everything. Everything settled like three weeks ago. My dirty uncle tried to get the money, but he failed. I had one of my friends run him off."

"Uncle?"

She lit another cigarette, stood, and opened the living room front window. Sat back down. "He's my mama's brother. One of the reasons we moved from Tennessee."

"Why?"

She became still. "You don't need to know about him."

He raped her. When she was a younger child. Did unspeakable things. Jesus. I don't want to know.

I picked up the softback textbook from the makeshift wooden table. "What's this?"

"Studying for my GED. Having a hard time making heads or tails of it." She grabbed the book from my hands, blew a stream of smoke toward the open window, where the draft sucked it out of the house. "So, who's you at the movies with? You got a girlfriend down at your fancy school in Hollywood."

I wondered how she knew I went to school in Hollywood, but I didn't ask. "I was with Rob and this other kid, Glenn. I got a scholarship to my high school. My parents couldn't afford it otherwise."

She changed the subject in an unexpected direction. "I heard about your cousin. Sorry."

A shiver rippled up my arms, and a pang struck at my heart. I studied my beat-up running sneakers. "It was my fault."

"Why?"

I explained the whole story to her, starting with my infatuation with Carrie Sullivan and sparing no detail, except I didn't rat out Peter. I told Annie about my visits to The Sprout, my encounters with the icy bogeywoman, Rebeccah. I told her how Cher had come home changed, unrecognizable. How she seemed disturbed, not in her right mind. I told her how I'd found Cher in the tub. And somewhere in the middle of that telling, I began to sob, and Annie knelt beside me with her arms around me, patting my back and saying, "Shh, it's alright, Stevie. It's alright."

126

"I killed her," I cried over and over.

"Shh. That woman killed her. I heard stories about her. That place did it. Not you. You couldn't know."

As Annie patted my back, Shpresa spoke. *She's right. It was Rebeccah.*

Shpresa had the strangest habit of poking her nose into things at times when her presence was the most unwelcome.

After a few minutes, Annie returned to her chair and began smoking another cigarette. I dried my eyes with my shirt and wiped the snot from my upper lip. My face warmed. "This'll give you something to tell them guys if they ever come around."

"They don't come around here," she snapped. "And if they did, I wouldn't say nothin' to them about you." A sly grin spread across her face. "But you know who does come by here?"

"Who?"

"Carrie Sullivan. And she's still cute as a bug's ear."

"Why would she come here?"

Annie chewed the inside of her cheek. "I got car payments and bills, and my grandma's Social Security stopped coming in full. I wait tables sometimes at the Tiki Torch down on Federal, but I don't make enough to live."

"I don't understand."

"I got a business going here, Stevie. Just grass. I don't play with that other shit."

I gulped. "Isn't that dangerous?"

"I got protection. Once I get my GED and get into community college, I'll move out near Davie, out west, and start over. Sell this house and get a small place out there."

"The people you sell for, they'll let you just leave?" I'd heard stories from Peter's father about how the mob, organized crime, supposedly worked. You didn't simply leave. The bosses didn't let you leave.

"I'll pay 'em off and go. I'm a nobody. They won't look for me." The tentativeness on her face suggested she wasn't sure about that. She stubbed out her cigarette. "You said your sister is gonna get you back, even after everything that happened?"

"I think."

"That's no shock. I told you not to screw with that girl, right? She's tough."

Takes one to know one.

"I know."

"You're book smart, Stevie. But you need a little common sense."

"Sometimes, maybe."

"Speaking of, I gotta get studying." She grabbed the book.

"Let me help you," I blurted.

"That's okay." A flush crept from her neck to her cheeks.

"Seriously, I'm going into Calculus this year, and I'm a junior. I probably know ninety percent of the stuff you need to know. Let me help you."

She ran her tongue across her top teeth. "What do you want?"

"Nothing? Think of it as payback for stealing your stuff."

"I already forgave you." She blinked. "You filled out nice, Stevie, but I ain't gonna fuck you. If I wanted to be a whore, I wouldn't be selling grass. It woulda been easier, and there's more money in it. Besides, I'm eighteen now, and you're jailbait."

I thought there might be a law that would make it okay for sixteen-year-olds to date eighteen-year-olds, but that was beside the point, so I kept quiet and studied our feet. Her pink toenail polish seemed to be even flakier than when I'd first walked into her house. Would I be able to say no if she asked me to sleep with her? I wasn't sure. Did I want to sleep with her? Maybe. Was that why I'd visited her house? No. I came because she was my friend and because I shouldn't have dismissed her so easily. And because of my nagging guilt, my need to somehow make things right. "No strings, Annie." I took the book from her limp hand.

"You know, I always gave you a hard time, but I also kinda liked you."

I wanted to ask her why, if she liked me, she had slept with Joey and Billy, but not me. I kept my mouth shut, though.

"But I got all caught up with Joey and Mr. Big Dick movie star." She meant Billy. She shifted in her chair. "What I'm sayin' is, you're alright, Steve. But I still ain't gonna screw you. I'll say hi to Carrie Sullivan for you when I see her, though."

I chuckled dryly and opened the book. "Ha, ha. Carrie Sullivan. Where do you want to start?"

I spent every other day at Annie's house for the next three weeks, helping her study. I'd call her, and she'd tell me when it was okay to swing by. Sometimes she'd make me leave quickly and walk around the block because she wasn't supposed to have anybody in the house when buyers came around and she sold them pot.

I expected studying to be a chore, but it flew by. Annie grasped the math concepts without me having to explain them twice. She told me I was a good teacher, better than the teachers at the high school, but I wondered if maybe she simply needed somebody to help her focus. I suggested some novels she might read, and she took me by the hand into her bedroom. My heart leaped, and she must have registered the change in my hand's temperature or my suddenly sweaty palms because she rolled her eyes, said, "No, dummy. I only wanted to show you this." She pointed to a small wooden bookcase on the wall by the door. The case was stuffed with books. She slid out a large novel, *Bleak House* by Charles Dickens, and proclaimed it her favorite: "This here was written by Charles Big-Fuckin'-Dickens." Then she laughed, and we cracked up. Who knew she was a reader? I'd never asked. I smuggled her books each week, starting with the first few novels in the *Time* quintet by L'Engle and ending with an older book called *The Awakening* by Kate Chopin. By the time Labor Day rolled around, I felt good about what Annie knew and how well she would do on the high-school equivalency test.

Early morning on Labor Day, she took a practice test. I scored it, and she passed easily. She squealed and hugged me, wrapping her arms around my neck and squeezing tight.

She drew back and we locked eyes, standing beside her cable-spool table. She leaned in until her lips met mine. We kissed slowly, our lips exploring each other, brushing, pulling back suddenly, coming together harder, sucking gently. The sexual tension I suppose both of us had been feeling as we'd studied across the last few weeks poured off us like hot grease sizzling in a pan. Her open kiss, her tongue curling around mine, still lit off fireworks in my mind. Both of us wore low-cut tank tops, and the tops of her breasts pressed warm against the skin of my chest. Her hands roamed across my back and down to my butt, whispering over my shorts, squeezing. The ends of my fingertips gently held her waist. I cupped one of her breasts, and she moaned softly. "You wanna go in my bedroom?" Her voice was breathy and hot in my ear.

"You still have furniture in there?" I murmured. "Or did you sell the bed since you showed me your bookcase?" She laughed, socked my arm, and tugged my hand, guiding me down her short hallway. "Take it on the Run" by REO Speedwagon played softly on her boom box in the family room as she and I made our way toward her bedroom door.

As I wondered if this was really happening, marveling at this spontaneous turn of events, Annie's kitchen phone rang. She dropped my hand and raced down the hall and around the corner to answer it. I poked my head out, checking on her as she listened to somebody on the

130

other end, closed her eyes, and sighed. "Okay." She hung up the phone, "Sorry, but you gotta go, Stevie. Don't come back today. It's my guy."

She never told me her 'guy's' real name, said it was safer that way. She either called him her guy or Danny. When her guy, the middleman distributor, visited, nobody else could be present in the house.

"I'll come back next weekend. We can, uh, pick up where we left off."

The expression on her face had gone flat, and the color had drawn back from the top of her chest. Her eyes darted about. "I don't know. We got carried away. Maybe it's not a good idea. You and me. You know?"

I stood with my hand on her doorknob. "Maybe not."

Why, oh why, did I say that?

My mother met me in the kitchen when I got home. "Where were you?" She tilted her chin up at me. "You weren't at Robert's. I was looking for you. Your father is grilling for Labor Day, and he needed you to clean the grill." The round-topped grill on the small patio, barely visible from over the top of the kitchen counter, hadn't been used for over two years, not since the summer Cher came to stay with us. "Were you at that girl's house? Don't lie. I saw you walking home."

"Girl?" I was prepared to lie, lie, lie about her.

"The one. The druggie."

I'd just about had it, and I made a mistake. The mistake of being too honest. "She's not a druggie. And I was helping her study."

Well, that lie ended quickly.

My father rose from his couch. "Study for what?"

He lives.

"Her GED. Her grandmother was sick, and she had to quit school to take care of her. Then her grandma died, and Annie inherited her house. She's studying for the GED so she can go to community college. She needed my help."

"She's paying you? Is that why you quit working at Wendy's again?"

"No. I did it as a friend. It was good practice for me too. To keep my mind sharp."

My mother got way up into my face. "You are not to go near that girl again. Do you hear me, Steven? I will not put another child into The Sprout if I can help it."

There it was. A not-so-veiled threat. "I'm starting school tomorrow. I won't have time to hang out with her. And she's taking the test soon anyway."

My mom shook her head. "So, help me, Steven."

So, help you?

"I'm going out to Winn Dixie to get potato salad. Help your father clean the grill." She stormed through the laundry room.

I went into the family room, and I lay on the love seat at a right angle to my dad. He turned on the television. *North by Northwest*, a black-and-white Alfred Hitchcock film, was playing. I'd seen this movie before. "Your sister's coming over." My dad's voice sounded lighter than it had in some time, almost happy. "Clean the grill in the next hour. Scrub it and rinse it out."

"Really? Marie's coming?"

"Yes. She was here earlier to say hello," my mother answered cheerfully from inside the laundry room where she had obviously stopped to gather her things.

Marie came over to say hello? To your mother? Check your bedroom!

"I'll be right back." I rushed to my bedroom, Shpresa's alarm bells ringing in my ears. She was right. My mattress was slightly off the frame, almost imperceptibly awry. It had not been in that position

132

earlier in the day. "What the heck? Did Mom do that? Marie? When was she even here to do that?" I mumbled. I closed my bedroom door and lifted the mattress, finding the packet of white powder.

My Dad's Biggest Surprise

Ironically, the best way to make a private call from my house in the afternoon was to close my parents' bedroom door and dial out using the black rotary phone on my mother's night table. After I found the packet Marie had stashed under my mattress, I ran into the backyard. Then I slipped into my parents' room and repeatedly spun my finger around their phone's old-fashioned dial, producing a satisfying feeling. Or maybe I was energized about the call I was making. The line buzzed, and my sister answered. "Hello?"

"I found what you left, Marie. I ran it out back, and now it sleeps with the alligators in the lake," I pronounced with a deep sense of pleasure.

"What the hell are you talking about, Steven?"

"You know exactly what I'm saying. The coke you planted. I tossed it into the lake. All the fish are swimming super-fast now."

Marie scoffed. "What a waste. You weren't even curious what it's like." A severe silence stretched over the line. "I was coming over in two hours to make a big show of discovering it. You got lucky, Steven, finding it when you did."

"After all this, you still want mom to send me into The Sprout? Do you know what that would do to Dad?"

Not to mention, do to me.

"It's called Narrow Line Academy now. Or something. And Dad wouldn't care. I don't think he'd miss you much at all."

Sadly, I believed she was right.

"No more Sprout? Academy? It's a school now?"

"Nope. Not a school. Maybe it's not called Academy. They say it's not as bad now. You'd be fine. Just two or three months out of your life. Julie Johnson said the worst person on the staff, a lady named Rebeccah Childs, is gone. She went to work in a rehab up north. I heard they hardly keep you up at night anymore. No more Christmas Carols. You'd be fine. Unless Simon's around."

"Well, your stupid plan to frame me didn't work."

"One way or another, little brother."

Vengeance is mine, sayeth Marie.

My sister is not God, Shpresa.

"Maybe I'll tell Mom and Dad about what you tried to do to me when you come over tonight for our Labor Day cookout."

"Cook out? Yeah, about that." The line clicked.

"Hello? Hello?" She was gone. How rude.

I made my way into the kitchen as the phone jangled. My father answered. "Hey, sweetheart!" His excited face grew stony. "I see. But I—" He stared at the handset. Did my sister cancel and hang up on him all at once? Wow, cold. My father, the corners of his mouth drooping, dragged himself to his couch where he lit a cigarette.

I plopped myself on the love seat, my hands in my lap. "I'll clean the grill now."

135

He removed his glasses and placed them on the glass coffee table, rubbing his eyes hard. "Don't bother." He sighed. "Marie's not coming."

"The three of us can still—"

"I said, don't bother." His tense growl, like a car revving, reminded me of how he used to sound when I was younger, right before he would smack me. I flinched as he rose and lumbered to the television. He flipped on *North by Northwest*, returned to the couch, and stretched himself out like a corpse, hands crossed atop his chest.

I reflected on the mostly gray stubble sprinkled on his face. A random question popped into my head. "How come you don't shave every day?"

"What?" His surprise at my question hung on his weathered visage.

"What I'm saying is, you shave like once every three or four days. Including today." I said this last bit even though I assumed he would have shaved soon if Marie still was coming over for the cookout. "Why don't you shave every day?"

His answer to my question rests in the vault of my memory, locked away but always there. It proved one of the most unexpected things I ever heard him say, and it marked the moment I started to both understand him better and worry about him. My concerns would prove justified. He said, and I quote: "I don't like staring at my own face."

Whoa.

"What?"

"Steven, the best advice I can give you is that a man needs to be able to look at himself in the mirror. You know I joined the war early, lied about my age." He was fifty-five, eight years older than my mother, and he'd joined up and fought in World War II in 1943 when he was sixteen going on seventeen.

"Yeah. So?"

"Well, war shows a man who he is. A man comes to understand when he's a coward at heart." He dragged on his cigarette, its smoke curling up to the ceiling like mist from a Satanic ritual. "So...I don't enjoy looking in the mirror."

Does my dad think himself a coward?

Yes, Steven. He does.

The room grew quiet except for Cary Grant's urgent voice on the television.

"You–you wouldn't send me to The Sprout, would you? Or whatever they call it now. I'm no druggie. I wrestle. I run. I do well in school. I don't do anything wrong." I was perilously close to whining, maybe because I knew I wasn't being entirely truthful. Early that summer, some of my schoolmates had thrown a beach party with a keg in front of the Hollywood Beach Hotel. We all had chugged a couple of beers too many. Rosie and I had slept it off under a monster beach towel on the sand. But he didn't need to know about that.

His sorrowful jowls appraised the television, and he stayed quiet. His non-answer smacked me on the side of my head: My sad father would do whatever my mother wanted, whatever she told him to do. He was worn away to less than a nub, like an eraser tip that had retreated into the green metal ferrule of a No. 2 pencil. No matter how well I behaved or how well I performed in school or at sports, he didn't care enough—didn't love me or himself enough—to fight my mother's craziness and give her anything less than what she demanded on any given day. My teeth gritted as he peacefully settled back to watching the television movie. I felt an odd, uncomfortable heat spreading from my cheeks down into my chest, a warmth connected to the metallic taste building inside my mouth. Even though, when I was small, my father sometimes lost his temper and lashed out, I'd never felt such a

137

simmering fury. It bubbled into a hot rage directed at him and his impotence. Rage at the world, too.

I clenched my fists. Without a word, I rose and marched to my bedroom. I slipped a record onto my phonograph—*Back in Black* by AC/DC. I ground my teeth some more, clenched my jaw. I wanted him to die. I wanted Rebeccah Childs to die. I wanted Marie to die. I wanted my mother to die. The song, "Back in Black," boomed into the room.

Did you want me to die, Steven? Did you want Cher to die? Do you want to die?

Shut up, Shpresa. Leave me be.

What do you want?

Revenge. For Cher. Revenge for everything. Control.

If you plan to murder someone for a crime, and you still blame yourself for that crime, Steven, then dig an extra grave. That's what they say.

I was just a dumb kid, Shpresa. My parents should have known better. I did the research on The Sprout at the public library a year ago. Congress said that place brainwashed kids like the communist North Koreans brainwashed people. How could my parents not know that? My deluded mother. My limp-dick father. Screw them, screw them, screw them.

Shpresa remained silent.

I won't come in hot, though. I'll wait until I'm cold. Like Marie. What's that saying, serve revenge cold?

I don't like where this is going, Steven. These horrible feelings will pass.

Will they?

I ate dinner in my bedroom, a bologna-and-cheese sandwich and potato salad. I made sure my school uniform was ready for the first day of school and shoved my workout clothes and wrestling shoes into a duffle bag, so I could work out with Chris and another teammate, Angel, late Monday afternoon while I waited for my parents to pick me up. I spent the rest of Sunday into the evening by myself, and nobody cared. Nobody noticed. Nobody bothered me. Nobody opened my door to catch the gleaming, burning, aching desire for vengeance in my eyes, to behold the craving for retaliation that beat inside my chest beneath my thin T-shirt.

I still felt that way in the morning when my parents dropped me off at school. And that's when I knew this feeling, though it might cool to a low simmer, would never leave me.

Dawn of the Dead

During my first week of school, as I got back into the groove of my schedule—academics, lifting, wrestling—I decided I wouldn't test my mother, so I would avoid Annie's house. Then, Sunday after church rolled around, Rob was busy, and I quickly broke that promise to myself by walking down there. I rationalized my visit by telling myself I should find out in person how she had scored on the GED exam. If I was honest, the prospect that we'd rekindle our spark and end up in her bedroom also played in the corners of my mind. And my mother was visiting a church friend, which made it easier to steal over there without the fear of getting caught.

I didn't call Annie first like I was supposed to do to ensure she wasn't busy with a deal. When I got there, no extra cars sat out front, though, only Annie's Pinto, so I figured everything was cool. I knocked, and nobody came to the door. The thought that something bad might have happened to her flashed through my mind. I knocked again, rapping harder. The door creaked open. Annie's light brown eyes blinked at me; her brows lowered. She swung the door wider, shot out her hand, grabbed my forearm, and yanked me through the doorway. "Get in here. Jesus, you're gonna get me in trouble."

A real-life zombie woman, like in one of George Romero's movies, stood in the archway between Annie's living room and her kitchen. The undead person clutched her rail-thin arms around her midsection. Her body, its skin sallow, was emaciated, bones threatening to poke through her flesh at the elbows and knees. She was barefoot and wore short, velour maroon shorts and a discordantly colored bright-red tube top that looked like it might fall off her smallish breasts. Her cheekbones carved dangerous shadows in her wan face, eyes deep-set within dark gray circles, like a sickly raccoon. Her greasy brown hair was tied back in a messy ponytail. She shifted from foot to foot, her nervous energy making me feel sick in my gut. She chewed at a nail on her index finger, and I imagined this ill creature munching on my brains. "Who the fuck is that?" the zombie-woman snapped at Annie.

"He's cool. He's a friend. It's cool," Annie assured her. My friend sat at her cable-spool table and weighed out a pile of marijuana, tying it in a baggie. She stood and handed the baggie to the zombie. "Ounce of Maui. It's forty. When's your guy coming back?"

The zombie pulled two wrinkly bills from her tube top and handed them to Annie. She shoved the baggie into her shorts pocket where it formed a noticeable lump on her upper thigh, like a tumor. "Soon. He'll be here soon. But that man shouldn't be here." The zombie pointed at me, her voice trembling with fear and disgust.

I was a man? I hadn't moved from the doorstep since Annie pulled me into her house and closed the door behind me. I cocked my head as I recognized the person this zombie used to be. "I know you. We went to church together."

The zombie did this weird thing with her teeth, baring them at me in an expression that barely resembled a smile and made her look

141

insane. Her teeth were yellowing like they hadn't been brushed for a while, and there was a black gap where one of her molars was missing. "I don't know you," she spat.

I did know her though. "Yeah, you know me. You're Julie. Julie Johnson. I'm Steve Jacobs."

The distressed girl began pacing from one side of the broad archway to the other. "I thought you said this guy was cool, Annie! He's not cool. He knows who I am. Not cool. Not cool."

Annie rubbed the girl's arm like she was petting a wild dog to calm it down. "It's okay. He is cool. He's fine. He works with me sometimes," she lied, graduating me to drug dealer status.

I was vibrating now at about the same frequency as Julie. That is to say, my heart was racing with anxiety. "It's okay, I hate The Sprout. They killed my cousin. It's cool." I don't know why I thought saying that would help her take a chill pill.

Julie spun and faced me from several feet away, her fists clenched and eyes shining bright inside their shadowy sockets. "What do you know about The Sprout, huh? They can call it whatever they want. It's a prison."

My throat had grown tight. "Yeah, but my sister says their staff changed. Like that lady, Rebeccah, she's not there anymore."

The girl's eyes widened, and a grimace stretched across her face. She seriously looked like a Muppet, a caricature of a human being. Annie had edged closer and began rubbing her shoulder again. "Relax, Jules. It's—"

"Rebeccah!" Julie screamed. I lurched back, and Annie dropped the girl's hand. The girl covered her own mouth with her hand. "Rebeccah," she repeated and giggled behind her hand as if she'd lost her mind completely. "She's still there. She's there. She's always there. Jingle bells, now you're dead, now you're gonna *die*," she sang the melody of

142

the Christmas song but with all the wrong words. She laughed, placing her fingertip to her lips. "Shh, Rebeccah's coming. Shh, be good. No, I wasn't asleep. Love tap. Love tap. We love you, Julie. We love you. Love tap." She swatted her hand in front of her face, slapping an invisible person.

"I don't understand."

"You said Rebeccah's gone? That's not right. They sent my little sister there, too, at the start of the summer. She called me, begging me to break her out. Crying about Rebeccah. That lady's still there." She squeezed her eyes shut and grabbed fistfuls of her own ponytail like she wanted to rip it from her scalp. "I couldn't help Janie because Rebeccah knows what I'm doing. All the time. She's in my head. She's in my head."

Good Lord.

Somebody knocked on the front door.

"Shoot." Annie scooted next to me, pushing me toward the hallway. "Hide in the bathroom, Stevie. Don't make a sound." I nodded.

Annie retreated to the family room, and I stared at her from the open bathroom door. "Jules, I'm going to answer the door. But the man in the bathroom isn't there. He was never here. Understand?" Annie grasped the girl's hands, pleading with her. I didn't wait for Julie's answer. I closed the bathroom door with a soft click. I pressed the lock, sat on top of the toilet seat, and wondered how I got to a place where I was cowering inside a bathroom.

The muffled sounds of a man's voice echoed through the house. Annie laughed. It sounded forced. There was some shuffling, and the front door closed. I waited. After about five minutes, Annie opened the bathroom door. "Come on out. What the hell, Steven? You're supposed to call first, man. That could have turnt out real bad. Hopefully, she keeps her mouth shut."

143

Annie and I sat in the plastic lawn chairs in front of the makeshift coffee table.

"Sorry. I–how'd the GED go?"

"I think I passed. I don't know yet." She lit a cigarette.

"What the heck was wrong with Julie? I heard she left home like a year or so ago. What's wrong with her?" I asked again. "She looked like the living dead."

Annie shook her head. "She's down in Miami and up to no good. It's a new thing."

"New thing?"

"It's called rock. This one guy calls it crack."

"Rock?"

"They take cocaine and dissolve it in a special solution. Then they boil the solution 'til it forms a rock. Then they put it in a glass pipe and smoke it. Instant high."

"That sounds...like it's not good."

She shook her head. "It's real bad stuff. Don't ever do it. *Ever.*"

"I've never even done coke."

"Good. Don't do that either. And for sure, don't ever smoke it. Jules and her pimp are down there in a house smoking it with a bunch of—"

"Wait, pimp? Julie's pimp? What?"

Annie dragged on her cigarette. "Yeah. That's the guy who dropped her at my house. Real mean dude. He'd turn me out if he could. They's up here in Lauderdale having a party, and they ran short on grass. He's friends with my guy, and he made an unannounced visit."

"Jesus."

"He'd like to have shot you if he found you here while she was buyin'."

"Jeez."

I sighed, chin on my fists, elbows poking into my knees. "Lot of good The Sprout did her."

"Yeah, right. You look like you could use a beer. Or a smoke."

"I can't do either because of wrestling."

She chuckled, took another drag. "Okay, jock strap."

I ignored her put-down. "I can't believe how bad she got in a year."

"Believe it."

"Annie, I–I don't think I can come here anymore. It's not that—"

"You don't need to explain yerself. I was gonna say, it ain't safe for you here. And I ain't gonna be here much longer anyway."

"What? Why?"

"My guy wants me to start selling rock with my grass. Like twofers. It's cheap, and it keeps people coming back. Wants me to be a halfway house for a whole bunch of the stuff, shipping it over to the neighborhood on the other side of Oakland Park Boulevard."

Glenn's neighborhood.

She shook her head. "It's not gonna happen. Them folks got enough trouble without me selling 'em rock. I got a buyer for this house, a friend of a friend. I'm gonna move in the middle of the night and keep a low profile. Leave my guy some extra money to take the edge off. He'll find somebody else to push his stuff."

I shook my head. "Sounds dangerous."

She shrugged. "Maybe. We'll see. But I got what I need to move on. I'm not greedy, Steven. That's the key to life. I just want to go to school, get a job, find a nice guy who doesn't cheat, and live my life with him. I like it out in Davie. Maybe, someday, if I get enough money, I'll buy a horse out there."

I hoped she was right. "This could be the last time we talk."

"Nah. We'll always be friends."

You may see her again, but you probably won't stay friends forever.

145

I know, Shpresa.

Annie and I both rose, and I moved to the front door. "I guess this is goodbye for now." I stuck out my hand. She eyed my hand, laughed, and wrapped me in a hug, squeezing me like she might never let me go. Her shampoo, the scent of apples in her hair, brought me back to sixth grade. Overwhelmed me. "Your hair always smells like apples," I murmured.

"Okay, take it easy, champ." She broke from our embrace and scanned me head to toe. "You be good to yourself, Steven." She bit her bottom lip. Was she about to cry? "Promise me you'll stop thinking about The Sprout. What happened to yer cousin wasn't on you. It's on them people. Don't think about that lady you and Jules was talkin' about. That woman's the bogeyman of South Florida, our own personal Jason. She ain't never gone get you, though. You're gonna have a good life, Steve Jacobs, or I'm gonna hunt you down and kick your pussy ass."

We both laughed thinly.

But Rebeccah will get other kids. That place, whatever they call it now, will get others.

As Annie swung the door closed, I said something I'd been wanting to say for a couple of years. "It was Peter."

The door halted midway in its swing, and she considered me, her expression flat. "That so?" She asked this question like she'd known the truth all along.

"He's not my friend anymore. Maybe he never was. I helped him. But it was his idea to take the pot. He was in on it."

"Hmm. Thanks for telling me."

"Don't hurt him," I begged as the front door swung shut.

I scarcely caught her last words before the door closed: "Don't worry. We won't hurt him too much."

146

Dead to Me

Sunday, December 12th, 1982

During wrestling season, Sundays were always the best day of the week, but some Sundays were better than others. During Christmas break, I slogged through two-a-day practices almost every day: I'd survive a grueling three-hour wrestling session in the early morning, sneak an hour or so nap on the spare Futon at my teammate Chris's house in the late morning, and return to my school for a 'lighter' two-hour practice session in the early afternoon. But Sunday was my one day off from practice, the day I didn't need to drag myself out of bed at five-thirty before the sun peeked over the flat horizon. The day I didn't have to haul my parents' car down I-95 to my high school's tiny wrestling room, where the walls would bleed sweat from the heat generated by my teammates and me.

And the second Sunday in December of 1982 proved even better than usual for two reasons. First, my team had won a Christmas tournament up in Lantana the day before, so our coach declared there would be no Monday morning practice. The next day-and-a-half would be practice-free. Second, not only was it my day of rest, but when I woke up and searched my house, I found it empty, my parents gone. They'd left me on my own, allowed me to stay home from church. Hallelujah! I figured my mother was pleased that I'd won all my consolation matches the day before to claim third place and help my team win the tournament. So, as a reward she'd let me skip church. After the finals, my coach visited my parents in the stands to congratulate them on my accomplishment, feeding their egos in front of the other parents. My mother ate it up—she only seemed happy in as much as my success reflected well on her.

I laughed to myself. Didn't my mother know she was treating church like a punishment, taking it away when I did something she deemed good?

After confirming my parents weren't lurking anywhere in the house, I sat on the edge of my father's sofa in the family room and stretched my sore arm. Something deep inside my shoulder clicked soundlessly.

That clicking doesn't seem good, Steven.

I know. But what can I do, Shpresa?

On Friday, after I'd lost a close match in the tournament quarterfinals to a tough wrestler from Naples, I couldn't lift my left arm above my head. Saturday morning, my shoulder felt better, and my coach taped it to my body, restricting its range of motion. I wrestled four consolation-bracket matches, winning them all to place third, and my school won the tournament by one point. The other good thing, my best friend from school, Chris, who was now ranked third in the 3A state at 142 by the Miami Herald, notched another tournament championship. Indeed, Chris's toughness, speed, and skill in the practice room were partly the reason for my success. I was only good because he was *great*, which forced me to work harder. The challenge he posed in the practice room, even though he was a weight-class below me, made almost everybody else that I wrestled seem easy in comparison.

I stripped in the hall bathroom and weighed myself, staring down at my skin and bones, the purple bruises flowering on my shins. The thin red arrow on the scale pointed to 152, only three pounds overweight even though I'd eaten a Whopper and fries from Burger King the night before as a treat. Not a problem. We didn't have another official meet until school came back in session in January, and at that time they'd give us a two-pound allowance. I headed to the kitchen to make myself two fried eggs and a piece of toast.

The phone rang, and I picked it up.

"You don't have ta' say nothin'. Just listen, okay." It was Annie.

"Okay."

"Yer folks there?"

"No, they went to church and left me here."

"Ah. Good. I woulda hung up if your mom answered." She paused. "How you doin'?"

"I feel like a truck hit me. Long tournament yesterday." I seriously felt like I'd drunk a kegger all by myself. "But I'm okay. It's my day off from practice. Maybe I'll snort some coke."

"Ha. Sure ya' will. I's reading the paper early this morning. You did good yesterday. Here's the headline: 'Marianist Marauders Powered by Halligan and Gryzbowski Surge to Win Santaluces Christmas Tournament.' The article says, 'Steven Jacobs battled through what appeared to be a mild shoulder injury to win third place and help secure his team's victory.'"

She had searched the wrestling results and found me. "Does it say that? That's cool. Yeah, it went well. Thanks." My left shoulder throbbed. I'd run later, but I'd pass on lifting weights or doing pull-ups.

"So, what's up?" Annie never called me at my house. We hadn't spoken to each other in over three months.

"You never asked me how I did on the GED."

"Oh, uh, well, you told me you were selling your house and moving. And anyway, I figured you were good. Right?"

"Yeah. I passed." She said this with a smidge of sadness as if I'd hurt her feelings for not calling to find out her scores, even though she had told me she was leaving town.

"Congratulations. I'm glad."

"Yeah, well, thanks for your help. I couldn't of done it without you."

"Nah. You would have been fine."

"Not true. But I called about something else."

"Hmm. What?" I cinched the phone's handset between my ear and my good shoulder while I popped a slice of bread into the toaster, tossed some butter into a hot pan, and cracked a couple of eggs. The eggs plopped with a sizzle into the pan. I grunted. My shoulder really hurt.

"You okay?"

"Yeah, my shoulder's sore. What's up?"

"I called to tell you to watch yer back. Some shit went down yesterday."

"Shit?"

"Yeah. I called Peter and Billy the other day. I told 'em I had some extra weed, and they could have it. Said I hadn't seen them in a long time so they should come over. Anyway, Peter came over but with Joey, not Billy. But I didn't have extra weed. I called Peter to scare him, and he took the bait. I had my guy there as protection. I told Peter I knew he stole my weed way back, that I heard him take it with you in my grandma's room."

"Whoa. What did he say?"

"He didn't admit it."

I cleared my throat. "I bet Peter knew you were bluffing. He and I were quiet when we did it, Annie. And you were busy at the time."

"I know what I was doin', thank you. Anyway, Peter got all mopey, but Joey started putting up a fuss, and my guy and Joey got in a fight."

"Jeez. Inside your house?"

"On my front lawn. Danny like ta' beat up Joey real good. Gave him two black eyes. Broken nose. Knocked him out. Wouldn't be surprised if Joey's jaw got broke."

"What did Peter do?"

She grunted. "Nothing. That pussy hung back and shot me dirty looks. He pulled Joey off the grass, and they ran away. They ain't coming back here. I shoulda beat Peter's ass myself. I probably could."

"You couldn't," I stated pragmatically. "And it would have caused bigger problems if Peter got beat up." I thought of Peter's dad. Joey's father owned a plumbing business, but Peter's father was another story.

"I know. I wish I could beat his ass, though. Anyway, Peter grumbled something about you as he was leaving. So, watch yourself."

"You know Peter's dad is in the Mafia or something, right?"

"Nah, that's just a rumor."

I gulped. "No, I don't think it is. His dad owns a concrete company or garbage company, but I don't think everything he does is legal. I think they own a big house on the beach up in New York. Or it's in one of his cousins' names. Maybe you should just let it go."

"Yep."

"Yep?"

"Yep, you're right. I'm gonna let it go. The wrong person got their ass kicked yesterday, but it's too late to fix it now. And you're right that maybe it's for the best. If Danny had laid out Peter, we'd be in a mess with his dad. And I'm leaving soon, anyway. That's why I called him over."

"You're leaving soon." A twinge pinched my heart. "I–I should come by and say goodbye."

"Don't."

I sighed. "I–I–good luck."

"That it? You ain't gonna invite me over to your house now?"

I couldn't tell if she was serious in her question. My parents would be at church for the next half hour, and I daydreamed about inviting Annie over to my house. I visualized us rolling together under my bed sheet, her underneath me, us moving together, kissing, doing everything. My thumb on her cheek. Her fingernails sliding down either side of my bare back. Me whispering 'I love you' to her…because I did.

Oh.

I did love her.

When did I fall in love with Analynn LeFevre?

About one week into helping her study for the test. When you realized she's about as bright as you are, but she never applied herself, never got the chance. Specifically, you fell in love as you were solving for X, and she leaned against you and patted your thigh. Or maybe it was when she said Bleak House was written by Charles Big-Fucking-Dickens. You're so easy, Steven.

My heart swelled in my chest, pumped up like a balloon. I thought all these things about Annie, felt all these feelings. What I said to her was: "Your friendship means a lot to me. Sorry that I haven't come by in a while, but I can't afford to get in trouble."

She laughed. "I'm a bad influence. I get it."

I changed the subject to sex, maybe because the image of making love to her had gotten lodged in my brain. But I totally said the opposite of how I felt. "You know, Annie, I'm glad we never did it." I wasn't sure why I said this.

"Hmm."

"You know what I mean?"

"Oh, I know what you mean. But why'd you say that? You finally get laid? Is that why you don't care about me no more."

I cared about Annie. If only she knew how much. Did she care about me? Did she love me?

Ask her.

No, Shpresa! Please, don't make me ask her.

Okay, have it your way.

"So, you finally did it with a girlfriend, right?"

How was I supposed to answer that? "Uh…" It happened after the homecoming dance. Victoria had driven us into a wooded area, steering her car down a dirt trail lit by headlights, a channel created by parked cars. Past the partiers—beers and joints in their hands—who leaned against their car hoods and whooped at us as we drove by, attuned to where we were headed. We drove way, way back to where the beehives sat. In the dark. Under a grove of trees with low-hanging branches. Ironically enough, we were west of Hollywood, somewhere near Davie. "Uhh…" I didn't want to tell Annie. It felt like I'd cheated on her.

"Ha! I knew it. Well, good for you. You still going out with her?"

"We broke up before the season."

An empty gap of silence stretched between us, and she spoke. "I'm glad we didn't do it. It would have gotten weird between us. We're better as friends." She sounded like maybe she didn't believe that.

"Exactly. Maybe someday."

"Stop," she breathed. Another awkward silence followed. "Maybe. But maybe not."

Maybe. Maybe you should tell her how you feel.

"You going to college next semester?" I asked her.

"Maybe."

"Where are you moving? Davie?"

"Steven, you turned out to be one of my favorite people. Who woulda' thunk it? You take good care of yourself." She dodged the question.

"You, too."

"Be good, Steven."

"You too, Annie."

"Bye, Steven."

The line clicked once, clicked again, and a rough voice replaced Annie's. "There you are. Your phone's been busy forever."

It was Peter. Shoot, my fried eggs were burning, the edges crisping to a nasty dark brown. I moved the pan off the hot coil, and I scraped the eggs onto a plate. Damn. Still edible though. I turned off the stove. My bad arm was pulsing with a dull ache. "Hey, Peter. What's up?"

"You know what's up, you fucking rat."

"What?"

"You ratted me out."

"I didn't think it mattered anymore. Whatever, man."

"Screw you, whatever. Joey got his ass beat because of you."

"Joey got his ass beat because he's a big mouth."

"Oh, so you know about it. You know what, man, you better watch your fuckin' back."

The acrid smell of burnt toast hit my nostrils. Our toaster dinged, and the blackened chip of bread popped up. Damn. I tossed the toast into the trash under the sink, slipped another piece of bread into the slot, adjusted the setting, and pressed the handle down to try again. "Whatever."

"He says whatever, again. You're dead to me, Steven. Be careful walking around the hood."

I'd had enough of this kid, to whom I hadn't said boo since I saw him at the movie theatre in August. "That so? Hey, you know what, Peter, forget you, too. My cousin would still be alive if you hadn't dragged me along to steal Annie's weed and left me holding the bag. So, really, go fuck yourself."

"Yeah, blame me for your cousin being weak and offing herself."

My temples throbbed, and hot blood warmed my cheeks. If I could jump through the phone and pound him to a bloody pulp...

"Weak?" The word rolled off my tongue like air, so soft, so hostile.

"You blame whoever you want, man. But be careful. Don't let us catch you alone outside, Stevie." The line went dark for a moment. "You're dead to me," he repeated.

"Yeah, you said that, Petey. Just...go away."

A click, and he was gone.

I stared at the handset.

You can't run in your neighborhood anymore. If they catch you running alone, they'll try to hurt you.

Yeah, it's only Sundays I usually run around here, anyway.

I filled a glass with water from the kitchen tap, sat, and ate my breakfast, thinking about my next move. After I wolfed down the eggs and toast, I called Chris's house, and his mother answered. "Hey, Mrs. H. Are you making your famous lasagna?" I was only half joking.

"I am," she stated without a trace of irony. "Are you coming over for dinner, Steven?"

"Maybe. Is Chris there, please?"

"He's still sleeping."

It was almost noon. "Any chance you can wake him, please?"

"Hold on."

After a long minute, Chris's groggy voice sagged through the line. "What the heck are you calling so early for, man? It's our day off."

"You running later?"

"Mmm, hmm. Of course."

"I'm gonna come down and run with you. Where you going?"

"Hollywood Mall. Sears."

"Come on, man. Somewhere else."

"Nobody's going to kidnap you, Steve," Chris snapped back with a hint of mirth, though the subject of his joke was grim. A young boy, Adam Walsh, had been abducted from the Hollywood Mall the year before, and it had made the national news. They'd found the poor boy's severed head up in Vero Beach, a hundred miles from Hollywood. "I'll protect you, man," he laughed.

"Screw you. You're too small to protect me."

Chris's father taught him Judo. He would thrash you in a fight.

I know.

"Ha, ha. I'm going at two. Come on down."

"Okay, my parents should be home in half an hour. I'll swing down around one thirty." My mouth watered thinking of his Italian mother's lasagna, one of the reasons Chris would show up to practice eight pounds over his weight each Monday. "Can I stay for dinner?"

"Are you seriously inviting yourself to dinner?"

"Come on, dude, your mom asked me if I wanted to stay. Also, we can swim after we run." In Chris's small, screened-in, heated pool, his dad, not a large man but some sort of black belt in Judo, would toss us around in the water like we were stick figures.

"Yeah, yeah. Why aren't you running in your own neighborhood?" he asked.

Because you're hiding, Steven. And running. Hiding from Peter, Joey, and Billy. Running from your parents. Running from your sister, even though she doesn't live at home anymore. Running down to Hollywood. Where it's easier, if not more fattening.

156

Shh, Shpresa.

"It's a long story. Some stuff in my neighborhood. I'll tell you when we run." I hadn't told him much about Annie or my neighborhood friends. Really, I hadn't told him any of the details about Cher and The Sprout and my mom. But maybe it was time. He knew my cousin had died and that it was a suicide. But he'd respectfully never asked the details. "It has to do with my cousin, Cher."

"Alright." I suppose my voice had turned serious because he answered in a solemn tone. "See you around one thirty. I'll ask my mom about dinner. There should be more than enough. Jackie's coming over for dinner." Jackie was Chris's girlfriend, who he'd been dating since freshman year. She was a compact, bubbling ray of sunshine, perfect for Chris's laid-back, affable nature. I didn't mind being the third wheel at his family dinner.

"Okay, I'll call Victoria and see if she can come, too."

"You're kidding."

"I am kidding. She and I have been done for a month."

"I thought so. You shouldn't have broken up with her. She was too hot for you."

"Fuck you. We'll run at two."

"Alright, kid."

That's how my best friend addressed me every now and then, as 'kid,' like I was forty years younger than him. And sometimes it felt that way. Sometimes I made believe that a select group of people in the world were reincarnated as themselves and lived their lives over and over, each time remembering their pasts. In my mind, Chris and Jackie fit this profile. They were teenagers, presumably like me, but they seemed like old souls, paradoxically filled at once with both gravitas and joie di vivre.

That's why, when I told Chris my story as we slowly jogged the first mile or so of our run—everything that I'd done, and everything that had happened since my original sin of stealing Annie's weed—he didn't say anything, merely nodded as if he understood. "That's some story," he said, finally, through his gasps for air, fingers laced behind his head after we'd sprinted up to the Hollywood Mall. That's all he said. No judgment.

Your story isn't over, Shpresa tickled the inside of my ear. *You've got more running to do, Steven.*

Shpresa was correct. I did have more running to do. I mostly stayed off my neighborhood's streets that winter, not even venturing outside to fetch the mail. I ran at Chris's house every Sunday afternoon over the break, including the day after Christmas. That Sunday, I arrived home at about five-thirty in the evening. I don't recall why I didn't stay at Chris's for dinner. My mom wasn't home. My dad sat on his sofa, head in his hands, crying.

The Notes

159

What My Dad Knew

Sunday, December 26, 1982

I approached my crying father with caution like I would a wild animal. His glasses sat on the glass coffee table in front of his sofa. He wore church slacks, and his spindly shins pressed against the low table as he hunched over, elbows on his knees and hands over his face. His shoulders shook, and his groans, 'ur-ur-ur,' were wildly out of place coming from him. I'd never seen him cry like this.

I lowered myself onto the love seat, facing him at an angle. "Dad," I said softly.

He startled and gulped, strangling his sobs. He dropped his hands from his face and appraised me with tear-stained, ruddy cheeks. "Steven. I thought you were eating dinner at Chris's house." He sniffed and wiped his eyes.

"No. Not tonight. What's happening?" For some reason, the notion that my mom had left him—left us—popped into my head. "Where's Mom?"

160

"At Cynthia Johnson's house." He shook his head and rubbed at his eyes again, sighing. "Do you remember Julie Johnson?"

Did I remember Julie Johnson? I remember how awful she looked the last time I saw her buying pot at Annie's. But it wasn't the pot that did that to her, that's for sure. It was rock cocaine. "Yeah. I think I remember her."

"She died."

I gasped. "Oh, my God. Was it drugs?"

"I don't know. Probably."

Probably, for sure. But why did he feel so bad about Julie Johnson, whom he hardly knew? I felt bad, off balance for a moment, but I knew it wouldn't affect me that much because I wasn't close to her. He must have seen the question in my eyes because he sniffed and said, "It made me think of Cher."

"Oh." I wasn't sure what to say.

Just listen to him.

Okay.

He licked his lips, wrestled his gold-rimmed glasses onto his face. "I should have fought your mother harder. We shouldn't have put Cher in that place."

I chewed the inside of my cheek, kept eye contact with him, and said nothing.

"I knew." His eyes welled with more tears, and his face scrunched.

"Knew what?"

"I knew those drugs I found were Marie's. I knew, and it's my fault. Cher was a good girl. I figured they'd see that and let her out." His lips pressed together and almost disappeared, the muscles in his jaw fluttering. "But they only wanted our *money*," he spat through clenched teeth. "I was on the phone with that rat bitch when I realized it was all about the money for them."

Every muscle in my body tensed in response to his sudden angry turn. My nervousness made me ask the only thing I could think of. "Who's a rat bitch?"

"The head woman. Howel's lieutenant, just a kid, really. Rachel? No, Rebeccah. Mr. Big wouldn't talk to us once he took most of our money. I tried to get Cher out, Steven. You've got to believe me. But they said they'd turn her over to the authorities. She might have gone to adult prison because she had turned eighteen. I don't know, maybe that's wrong. Maybe they bluffed me." He held his head in his hands again. "What a mess I made. And then, she couldn't take it anymore. I should have sued those bastards, but I just took it. I just took it from them. I'm a coward all the way home. All the way home." He began to sob again, head hanging low, and I wanted to go to him, to wrap my arms around him. But I blamed him, too, now even more than before. I blamed him as much as I blamed myself. So, I sat motionless on the love seat, a slick rubber ball of sickness bouncing about in my gut. "I shouldn't have let them take Cher or take anybody. I should have fought your *mother*." He landed hard on the word, 'mother,' then sniffed once.

I tried to say something wise. "What's done is done, Dad. Marie's alive. I'm alive."

Thank God.

He sniffed deeply once more and rubbed his reddened eyes. "Marie won't talk to me."

"She loves you."

He simply shook his head, staring at his black socks.

She's his favorite child.

I know. Thanks for the info, Shpresa.

"She does love you, Dad."

"She won't come here because of your mother."

"We—we're all responsible for what happened to Cher." Desperate to soothe him, I took a wild chance on the truth, assuming at this point he would never let my mother put me in The Sprout, or whatever they were calling it these days. "One of those baggies was mine."

His eyes widened, but he said nothing.

"I was holding it for a friend. I didn't smoke it. I'd only ever done it once. But Marie moved her stash because I let it slip that I knew where she kept her stuff, and that's why you found the drugs. So, it was all of us. And maybe Marie should have gone into that place, I don't know. But it's the people at that place who are to blame. What did they do to Cher in there?" I truly wanted to know.

He shook his head. "You were the last one we suspected." His voice was so small, incredulous.

"Sorry to disappoint you."

"You're not doing anything now, though, right?"

"No."

Not during wrestling season anyway.

Shh, Shpresa.

He sniffed a third time. "We're proud of you. Proud of Marie. She's doing the best she can, making good money bartending at Penrod's. School was never for her. She'll be okay."

"Marie will always be fine," I assured him. I believed that. My sister was the type of person who always landed on their feet.

"It hurts my heart sometimes, Steven, thinking about Cher. She deserved better. It hurts my heart."

I nodded. She did deserve better. She didn't deserve what she got.

"So, you're not going to put me in The Sprout?"

"No. Not in a million years." He laughed, and I let out the deep breath I'd been unconsciously holding. As long as my father had a say, I didn't have to worry about getting sent to that nasty place ever again.

Alongside my relief, I felt something else blossom like a lump of small white-hot coal inside my chest: irritation. Soreness that he had allowed such an awful thing to happen to Cher. He was the grown-up. The guardian. He was supposed to protect her. My mother was a fool, but he was weak. He'd been too weak to do right by my cousin. Or even to attack those bastards at The Sprout afterward when they sent Cher back to us shattered. I rose from the sofa and went to my bedroom before I said something stupid.

But, still, my chest was light with relief. Marie couldn't touch me. My father wouldn't let the awful things that had happened to my cousin or Julie Johnson happen to me. For the first time in a long time, it felt like things were on the upswing. I swirled my shoulder, making a large circle in the air with my arm as I strode down the hall to my room. Over the last week, my arm had started to feel better, miraculously healing itself amid the intensity of the wrestling season. I shoved my anger at my dad down into the bowels of my chest. My life was good. I should be happy. He wouldn't make the same mistake twice, and he would protect me. Everything would be okay…

The Forgery

Three days later, on Wednesday, December 29, 1982, two years to the day that I found Cher limp in the hallway bathroom's blood-soaked tub, my father died.

When I found him, for an instant, I thought he had gone the same way as Cher and tried to kill himself. He was alive, lying flat on the couch in his boxers and a dirty white T-shirt. His eyes were squeezed shut, and he was wheezing like a wounded horse and clutching his left arm. A rumpled piece of looseleaf paper lay on the coffee table beside him, and the kitchen phone handset dangled by its cord over the counter, hanging near his head.

I ran to him and knelt. "What's wrong?"

He managed a hoarse whisper. "I called 911. Your mother took a cab to Cynthia's." Then he groaned and grasped at his chest through his T-shirt. His face turned purplish, he moaned again, and his arms went limp at his sides, his body slackening.

No, this couldn't be happening. "Dad?" I shook his shoulders. Nothing.

"Dad? Oh, Jesus!" I put my ear next to his mouth. No air was coming out.

I started pressing on his chest, the way people did on television. I wasn't sure I was doing anything, and afterward, I couldn't recall how long I tried to revive him. I didn't remember hearing the ambulance people rush into my house either, but suddenly there they were, pulling me from him, strapping a plastic mask over his face, squeezing air into his lungs with a plastic contraption, and pumping on his chest.

When I had entered the house, I had slipped off my sandals by the front door. Now, my bare big toe touched the piece of looseleaf paper, which had drifted to the floor. I picked it up as the emergency workers tried to revive him. I was numb to everything happening around me, wondering if I should be doing something. They dragged the coffee table out of the way, slid my father onto a gurney, which rose as if by magic, and wheeled him out of the house as one of them continued to pump his chest. One of the men, who wore a dark blue uniform with a red-and-white patch, got into my face. "Can you drive that car out front?"

I must have nodded yes.

"Go to Holy Cross Hospital," he said as he shut the front door.

I nodded again, though now I was alone. I thought of my mom. I needed to reach her. The people were out of the house now. Everything was quiet, completely still as if none of what just happened had really occurred. As if the last several minutes had been a nightmare, and now I was awake in my still, still, still house.

Cynthia Johnson's phone number is in your mom's address book. On her night table. Or in the drawer.

Still feeling like a bubble had swallowed my head, I staggered down the hall, the piece of looseleaf paper hanging limp between two fingertips. I sat on their King bed, and I stared down at the paper in my hand, at my dad's chicken scratch:

I think I'm having a heart attack. I might die. Linnea I love you and Marie and Steven. I love you all even if I didn't always know how to show it. I'm glad I married you. I'm glad we raised a family. I am so guilty so guilty about Cher. I knew it was Marie but I let you convince me to put Cher in that place with those bad people. They killed her. We killed her. I let her die I killed her. God is punishing me I know it because I knew those drugs were Marie's. We should have put Marie in rehab she would have been fine because she's strong. I should have threatened them to get Cher out. I love you but if I die you need to know this. I called the ambulance but they don't seem to be----

His handwriting turned illegible after that and ended in a scribble. The note was unsigned.

I walked to the kitchen and grabbed another piece of looseleaf paper from the drawer beneath the phone, where my dad probably obtained this sheet. I sat the pieces of paper side by side on the counter and studied his handwriting. Then I forged another shorter note, repeating the things he said about loving us but leaving out the stuff about Cher and Marie.

I crumpled the paper to make it look more realistic, smoothed it out, and dropped the fake note on the coffee table in front of his sofa, its cushion still indented.

I folded the real note and slipped it beneath crepe paper inside a shoebox that I shoved way underneath my bed. I knelt at my bed, closed my eyes, and said a prayer for my dad, hoping he would be fine. He would be fine. He had to be fine. Then I headed back to my mother's room to find Cynthia Johnson's number.

By the time Marie, my mom, and I converged at Holy Cross Hospital, they informed us my dad was gone. They said he died in the ambulance, but in hindsight, I suspected he died in our house. I'd seen him go limp, witnessed the exact moment the breath had left his body. Not that it mattered much where it happened.

After the hospital, at the house, as the three of us sat dazed, not quite accepting yet that he was gone and never would come back, Marie grabbed the note I'd written and left on the coffee table. My sister took it in, her eyes darting toward me every so often as she read. She let my mother read it, and then ripped it from her hands. In doing so, Marie tore the paper in half just below the signature. My sister hurried out of the house with the fake note in her hand. Just as quickly, she ran back inside to us, handed the note to my mom, mumbled, "You can have this garbage," and rushed back out.

At the funeral, I remanded myself for ever having thought Marie was a sociopath like Ted Bundy. Her soul had been pierced like somebody had taken a pair of scissors to her heart and gouged it out. I'd never seen my sister cry so hard. She really loved my dad, maybe because she was his favorite. It amazed me how I never knew the depths of her emotions for him. But death is like that—it often reveals deeply hidden truths. At my father's graveside, Marie hugged me long and hard, but she wouldn't look directly at me.

My mom, well, God works in mysterious ways, and my mom was convinced my dad was supposed to die when he did. She concocted a narrative that God was doing all this for some unimaginably wonderful purpose. To make us strong maybe. But in her view, it was not our job to question how or if this situation would become extra wonderful. She built an optimistic religious story to fit the events, and that was that.

Me? When we viewed my dad before the funeral, I found myself surprisingly overwhelmed with sorrow, like a switch had been flipped. I cried over his body, surprised at how cold his forehead was when I kissed it, and shedding half-angry tears that he hadn't loved me better. I promised him, in my mind, I would do better than him if I ever raised a family. Like it was an easy thing, raising a family. What did I know about that? I didn't cry afterward at the actual service. I didn't feel much of anything by the time the funeral rolled around, and I wondered if there was something wrong with me.

At the funeral on Monday, two days after the new year, people kept asking me how on earth I got the split lip and black eye, which at that point had turned more yellow and purple than black and blue. I smiled politely at their questions. How I got hurt was nobody's business. Not my mom's concern. Not Marie's. Not anybody. It was between Annie and me. As far as anybody else knew, I fell off the front porch or stumbled over the lip between the family room slider and the patio. Only I knew that I had gotten what was coming to me. It was that simple.

How I Got a Black Eye and Split Lip

Friday, December 31, 1982, 2 AM

My mother's voice hissed into my ear in the dark, her sharp fingernail poking my shoulder. "Steven. Steven. Wake up. Was that one of your friends? Why are we getting prank calls at two in the morning?" She loomed above me, a murky, faceless demon in the swirling shadows of my bedroom. She could have been the devil for all I knew.

"What? I don't...Why are you waking me up? I'm sleeping." I stated the obvious, clutched my pillow tighter, and rolled away from her to face the wall.

She tapped my shoulder again. "If you know who it is, I want to know. We *will* talk about this when you wake up, Steven."

A threat, not a promise. Maybe both. "Tired," I muttered groggily, wiggling my body rebelliously, still facing the wall. "Go to sleep, Mom."

"I can't sleep. I've been up all night. I've got a million things to do before the funeral Monday."

She said this, and it flashed into my head that my dad, honest to God, died yesterday. In front of me. An icy hand gripped my heart,

170

twisting it inside my chest. It was true. He was gone. I recollected the dream I'd been having before my mother woke me up. My wrestling buddy Chris and Annie were calling me on the phone from another room in Annie's house. At the start of the dream, I walked in on them naked in Annie's bedroom. Chris lay with his back against Annie's headboard, and she sat on him atop the sheets, the back of her dirty-blonde hair facing me as she rocked up and down, moaning. The headboard knocked against the wall, thump-thump-thump, like it did the day Peter and I heard Billy and Annie doing it behind closed doors. Because Chris and Annie were on top of the sheets, I could see everything, and I found myself, at once, disgusted and aroused. I was horrified because Chris loved Jackie, and I wondered how he could do something so shockingly awful to his girlfriend of two years by cheating on her with Annie. Not to mention that Chris had never even met Annie in real life. I told Chris I was disappointed in him, and he replied, "I'll have sex with whoever I want when I want, kid. Go into her grandma's room and we'll make a phone call to you to explain." He said that, and in a snap, I sat cross-legged on the bed in Annie's grandma's room, stacks of newspapers stretched to the ceiling, a towering maze around me. In my lap, I stroked a black rotary phone like a kitten. The phone rang and rang, and I stared at it, paralyzed and unable to answer. The ringing ended, and Chris's muffled voice called my name from Annie's bedroom, and that's when I woke up to my mom prodding my shoulder and calling my name.

My mom was gone now, leaving my bedroom door open. She shuffled down the hall, a ghost in her light pink bathrobe, her blonde locks lit by the soft glow of the kitchen lights at the house's other end. I sat up in bed. Had somebody called our house at two in the morning and then hung up?

Annie! It must have been Annie.

171

Annie was in trouble. I recalled that she once told me if she ever called my house and my mom answered, she would hang up.

I closed my door and dressed, slipping into a beat-up pair of sneakers, I slid open my window. I'd removed the screen from the frame years ago in case I ever needed to make a quick exit, although I'd never snuck out until now. I scrambled through the window, glad there were no bushes underneath as I dropped to the thick-bladed South Florida grass. I jogged briskly out of the cul-de-sac and down the street toward Annie's. The night air was warm and thick, and I wiped a thin line of sweat from my brow. I stopped and spun around when I thought I heard something behind me, but there was nothing, nobody there, only the shadows, and the softly glowing streetlights. I conjured up the image of a serial killer following me like in the movie, *Friday the 13th*.

Annie's house was closed-up, quiet. Its muted porch light struggled to cut through the night. It felt like the darkness was threatening to escape the field on the other side of the street, float across the asphalt like an inky fog, and rise to swallow her house. Another noise, maybe a cracking twig, broke the night. I checked over my shoulder. Nobody there. I tapped on her bedroom window, which was in the front on the right. "Annie."

There was no answer, and I tapped again. The corner of her blind edged open, and Annie's tanned face, alarm in her eyes, peeked out. She signaled me to head to her front door.

I met her at the front door. She was wearing white pajama shorts and a short-sleeved pajama top, which could have been pink or peach, hard to say in the porch light. "What the hell, Steven?" she whispered. "You're gonna wake my neighbors."

"You called me earlier, right? Like twenty minutes ago," I replied, my voice also low.

She shook her head. "Nope."

There was a crunching behind me, the sound of Bermuda grass underfoot. I spun. Peter stood like a ghoul in the middle of her lawn, barely visible under the porch light's dim glow. "Nah, that was me that called you." He kept his raspy voice low. Joey stood behind him on Annie's driveway.

He tricked you. They're not here to talk.

I know, Shpresa, thanks for nothing. I figured it out.

I sized them up. Peter had gotten taller over the last couple of years. He was slim and athletically built, but he was still an inch shorter than me. If I could get my hands on him, I could probably handle him. But I couldn't manage him and Joey at once if they both attacked me. I scoffed. "You need to do this two-on-one? Can't you handle me by yourself, Petey?" There was going to be a fight, but I wasn't scared, not even a little nervous. I marveled at the difference between my calm reaction as a sixteen-year-old and the jangle of nerves that would have rattled around the chest of twelve-year-old me or even fourteen-year-old me.

"Nah, I don't need anybody's help. Joey's just here to make sure things are fair."

"You dumbasses should go home," Annie hissed.

"Shut up, hillbilly," Joey barked.

"I'm a redneck, not a hillbilly, asshole. There's a difference."

"Let's go, Stevie," urged Peter, still on the front lawn. He squared off with me, his arms jacked out from his sides aggressively. Joey remained poised on the edge of the driveway as if the front lawn represented the ring and he was, at least momentarily, respectfully spectating from the sidelines.

"I got this, Annie, don't worry." I moved toward Peter.

"This is stupid." Annie huffed. "I don't need this problem."

I raised my fists, and Peter raised his. This was happening. We circled. I planned to hit him with a double-leg takedown the moment I got an opening. His right fist jabbed out, connecting with my mouth, snapping back my head. My mouth grew numb and then ached where he'd struck it. His hands were fast. I couldn't stay on my feet with him for long, or he'd box me to shreds. I brought my fists tighter to my chin, and I feinted with a mock punch. As his hands flinched to block, I shot underneath him, a perfect wrestling penetration step. It proved easier to take him down and keep him on the ground than I thought it would be. I had been trained to take people down and keep them down—to pick their ankles, chop their arms, control them with my arms and legs…to frustrate, frustrate, frustrate, deny, deny, deny—and Peter knew nothing about fighting on the ground. But I couldn't bring myself to hit him, even though at one point I could have showered blows on the back of his head. I wasn't angry at him anymore, and I didn't want to hurt him. My heart told me Cher wasn't his fault. I'd swallowed all the blame for that. I had no rage left for Peter, only guilt for myself. I'd ratted him to Annie because she deserved to know who stole her stash, but I felt none of the anger or even determination I channeled when I typically wrestled a match. I went through the motions of keeping him down in a tired, lazy manner, a sadness aching in my chest. He was a toy beneath me, and I pitied him.

Where does this end? I thought as I shoved Peter's face into the grass, for an instant fooling myself that Shpresa had spoken to me. *If I beat him up, does his father get involved? At what point does Joey, who's out of my line of sight, kick me in the back of the head?* I caught Annie in the corner of my eye, standing on her porch in her bare feet, hand clutching her own throat. *At what point does this fight blow back on my friend? She's got enough trouble. Annie deserves better.*

I'd thrown in my legs on his legs, riding his back like a cowboy and pressing his head down. His hand was flat on the grass, and I imagined placing him in a Judo hand lock like Chris's father had taught us. I could have done it. But what if I injured him? His dad was in the mob, and it would never be over if I did that. Suddenly, I knew what I had to do. I shifted my weight, so I rode slightly high on his back. *Come on. Come on,* I thought. *Do it. Do. It.* He took the gift, shrugging me over his shoulders. I tumbled to my back on the grass, and Annie cried out. He took the advantage I gave him, scrambling on top of me, knees on either side of my chest, raining blows at my face. He landed a solid punch on my eye—ouch—before I could wiggle out from under him, scramble away, and curl up like a bug on the grass. "I'm sorry, man!" I whined, my hands defensively covering my face and head. "No more, please. Please, man, I'm sorry," I pleaded as if he'd tromped me but good, playing to his ego. "Please."

He stood over me and kicked my ribs.

Ugh. What a dick. That was going to bruise. But I deserved this. I deserved worse.

"That's what you get, you rat. Come on Joey." The grass crunched as Peter, victorious, stomped toward the driveway.

My two ex-friends chuckled, and Joey shouted something crude at Annie, something horrible about her private parts that I would never repeat. It made me want to leap off the grass, rush Joey, and hip-toss him to the asphalt, but I stayed down. This needed to end here.

Their laughter rang through the night as they ambled like two raucous carefree bumbling scarecrows into the pitch-black field. For some reason, they were heading away from the neighborhood. Maybe they were planning to take the long way home, up Twenty-first Avenue and through the apartment complex adjacent to the back end of our neighborhood. Who knew? They vanished from sight, and their laughter dissolved into the gloom. Then Annie's hand was under my armpit, tugging me up. "You okay?"

I wiped my bottom lip, and my finger came away dark and wet. I was bleeding, but not much. "I'm fine. Maybe I could use your bathroom." A light snapped on in her neighbor's window, and the blinds parted. A pale face peeked out at us.

"Come on. Before they like ta' call the cops." She kept her shoulder under my armpit and her arm around my waist as she guided me into her house.

"You don't need to carry me," I chuckled. "I'm a big boy. I can walk myself."

"I know." She sat me on top of the covered toilet seat and pulled a bottle of hydrogen peroxide from her medicine cabinet.

"Nooo. I don't need that crap."

"Well, I gotta clean it with somethin', ya' wuss. He gave you some shiner." She traced the tip of her index finger over the small bump on my eyebrow, and I closed my eyes. There was something tender and sensual about her touch, regardless of the situation. "I got wipes. Here." She put the hydrogen peroxide back into the cabinet, knelt by me, and ripped open a small packet. "Keep your mouth shut. Dirt got into this cut on your lip." The smell of alcohol wafted into my nostrils as she gently wiped my swollen, sore bottom lip. It stung a little, and I tried to embrace the pain and not flinch. She spoke to me as she swabbed the cut. "You're ranked number six in Florida at 149, did you know that? The new 3A and 4A high school rankings came out in the Sentinel today. Did you know that?" she repeated as she cleaned my tiny wound. I shook my head, no. "Be still," she chided me. How did she expect me to answer her if I couldn't talk or shake my head? "But you fell off the top of that dickwad and let him get on top of you like you didn't know nothing about nothing. So, what the hell was that?"

"Hmm." I shrugged. There was no easy answer to her question.

She squinted, studying her work. "Perfect. All the dirt's out."

I wish all the dirt was out.

"You decided it weren't a good idea ta' whoop his ass. You think yer protectin' me?" She sounded more Southern, and I figured it was because she was excited.

I sighed. "I guess. It was better that it ended like this. I've known him a long time, and he's got no killer instinct. I knew he wouldn't hurt me bad. And you said yourself that you can't afford trouble."

A funny look flashed across her face, and she tilted her head. Then she leaned in and kissed me, her closed lips lingering on mine. As she pulled back, a drop of moisture remained on my throbbing bottom lip.

I sat squarely on the toilet cover, and I visualized her kissing me again and climbing on top of my lap, her smooth tanned thighs on either side of my legs, her tongue swirling in my mouth. I would caress her earlobe with my thumb and trace my fingers down her neck, across her clavicle, and lower to caress her breasts. I'd rub her bare thigh, and she would squeeze my shoulders. We'd struggle to take off our clothes, and...

She was smiling at me, simultaneously studying my face and the rest of my body. "It's just a kiss. What the hell is goin' on in your head?"

I exhaled hard. "Kissing me defeats the purpose of cleaning my lip, doesn't it?" I folded my arms across my crotch, trying to conceal the effect of the heady craving flowing through my body, filling my soft spots with lustful blood and deepening my breaths.

She blinked. "Maybe you should go, Steven."

Ugh. No. Please.

"Only if you want me to go."

Her peach pajama top—it was peach, not pink—was undone to the third button, and the top of her bare chest flushed. She paused for what felt like an eternity. "You should go, Steven. You don't wanna get caught out this late by yer mom."

I rose, all the while wondering what was holding her back. "Okay."

She walked me to the front door and opened it. "Thanks for being such a wussy tonight. I got too much goin' on ta' worry about that dickweed givin' me trouble. Anyway, thanks."

Maybe she's got too much going on to worry about you, Steven. Maybe her sending you home is not about you at all. Sex complicates things. Especially when feelings are involved. She knows that.

Sometimes, Shpresa, I hate you.

"Okay." I couldn't believe I was leaving, and I didn't know what else to say. I wanted to pick Annie up, carry her to her bedroom, and make love to her. Whisper into her ear that I loved her.

You should tell her at least. How deeply you care for her. I've told you this before.

No, it wouldn't do any good.

Suit yourself.

"Bye, Steven. Love ya'," she said to me as she shut her door.

"Love you, too," I replied, but I didn't think she heard me as the door clicked shut.

Four nights later, the night after my father's funeral, I snuck out of my bedroom window and scurried through the neighborhood to see her. I planned to tell her how I felt, to empty my heart to her.

Her driveway was empty, the Pinto missing. The blinds were absent from her bedroom window in front. I peeked inside. The bedroom was vacant. Nothing remained—no bed, no dresser. She was gone.

She would get in touch with me, I figured. Send me her phone number or her new address, somehow. But Analynn never told me where she went to live. She simply went away and didn't come back.

Nowhere to Run

Friday, December 31, 1982, noon

My mom was gone when I woke up on New Year's Eve. It was just as well. I don't think she would have believed I rolled out of my bed in the middle of the night and gave myself a black eye and split lip. But if she returned home later in the day, she would assume I'd gotten into a fight that day, not the night before. I figured she had gone to church to pray—to pray for my dad, to pray for us. I wrinkled my nose at the thought. What good would her praying do? He was gone, and that was that.

She does care about you. Is it so bad that she prays? Shpresa asked as I dug into a bowl of cornflakes. I neglected to answer her. *You prayed for your dad, Steven. Or did you forget?*

True. True.

I lolled around my house most of the afternoon. My wrestling coach called to let me know they were all thinking of me and praying for me, and to inform me that I didn't need to come back to practice until after my father's funeral. They were canceling practice Monday, and most of

180

the team planned to show up at my father's wake. I told him thank you and said maybe I'd try to attend Saturday's post-New Year practice. "I'll run to keep in shape, coach, don't worry." I laughed as if it mattered. I swung my left arm in large circles as I spoke to him. The clicking inside my shoulder had returned since my fight with Peter.

I hung up on my coach, and the doorbell rang. Peter's youngish mother, her attractive face now bleak, stood on our front stoop. For a moment, I thought she had shown up at our house because of my fight with her son, but she held a glass casserole dish covered with foil. Lasagna, she said, because we shouldn't have to cook. She was there because of my dad. I thanked her and took the warm dish, facing off with her awkwardly in the doorway, not sure if I should invite her in since my mom wasn't home. I told her my mom was at church, but I'd let her know she left the lasagna. She narrowed her eyes as she checked my face, and I hoped she didn't know my bruises were her son's handiwork. Did her boy sport grass burns on his forehead or cheeks from when I shoved his face into the ground? If so, I hoped she didn't connect the dots and figure out we'd been fighting.

Across the early afternoon, my mom didn't return from wherever she had gone. Two more women, both from our church, came by with dishes of food, which I put into the fridge. I stood in front of the closed refrigerator, shut my eyes, and repeated in my head: *I will not eat this food. I will not eat this food.* Then I went for a run, mostly to avoid picking at the tempting kugel, which smelled of raisins and noodles and heavy cream.

My skin dimpled in the cool air as I ran. The temperature was in the upper fifties, the air as dry as possible for South Florida. I jogged through the neighborhood toward Prospect Road. Billy stood outside his house with a green hose in his hand. Was he watering his front lawn? Weird. He tossed me a chin nod. Really? Okay. "Hey, man," I said, upping my pace as I passed him. When I got to Prospect Road, I turned right, east in the direction of the beach, and I sprinted, maybe a sub-six-minute-mile pace, all the way to Powerline Road. At Prospect and Powerline, I jogged in place, staring at the massive gray columns supporting the raised highway, I-95, which crossed over the road near the intersection. Chris told me once that the highway went all the way up the coast to Maine, that if I ever wanted to leave Florida and go somewhere else on the east coast, that was the way to go. Not today, but the path out was there when I needed it. I spun, and I ran toward home.

When I reached the entrance of my neighborhood, I got an idea. I passed my neighborhood, ran up to Twenty-first Avenue, and jogged south on Twenty-first in the direction of my sister's apartment. I wasn't sure exactly where she lived, but after a half hour of running in and out of neighborhoods, I found her apartment complex. She and Rick lived on the second floor of the front building. I rapped on her door. She answered right away, almost as if she'd been standing by the door waiting for me. She wore pajamas still, and her eyes were bleary, filled with thin, squiggly red lines like she'd been crying. Her usually perfectly styled blonde hair poked out in odd-shaped tufts from her head. She sniffed, left the door open, and turned around, a wordless sign for me to follow her into her apartment. I sat in a beige-cushioned chair with a bamboo frame in her tiny living room, and she dropped into a matching chair beside me.

"You doing okay?"

"No. I'm not," she answered flatly.

We stared at each other for a few torturous moments.

"I tried to save him," I said weakly, thinking maybe this would make her feel better. Or make her feel better about me.

"I heard. You did what you could." She crossed her arms.

I was unsure what else to say to her. I scanned her apartment, which had a tropical theme, a covered parrot cage in the corner. "Nice place."

She scoffed. "You've been here before."

She was right, but I was only trying to be pleasant. With some people, you never can do or say the right thing, though. "Why are you always so mean to me, Marie?" Couldn't she be nicer today? He was my dad, too, after all. I hurt, too. She had to know that.

She played back my words in an exaggerated, whiny squeal: *"Why are you always so mean to me, Marie?"* She tsk'd and mumbled, "Little baby."

I sighed.

She gazed at me without expression. "Why do I act mean to you? Because I can."

Wow.

"Are you coming over tonight? Mom said you might."

"I might. I don't know. Just because Dad's gone doesn't mean I want to be around that woman."

"What did she ever do that was so bad?"

"You're kidding, right? She listens to nobody. She cares about nobody," Marie grumbled.

Your sister is more like your mother than she knows.

I know. I'm just noticing that. What's the word?

Intractable.

"Why are you here, Steven?"

"I–I was running. I realized I was in your apartment complex. I wanted to see…"

I've got nobody else to run to. Is that enough, sister?

"I love you, Steven." She sniffed again. "But you're not out of the woods with me yet."

"Really, Marie?"

"You would have let them—let Mom put me in The Sprout. You're the reason all this happened. All this starts with you. So, yeah, really, Steven."

Is she blaming me for Dad's death? As if I didn't feel guilty enough.

She continued, soft and low, emotionless. "I'm still going to get you back. And when I do, keep your cool. Don't fail."

What the hell? "I'll be seventeen in three months, Marie. What are you going to do to me?"

She didn't answer me.

There was nothing more to say.

You should leave.

Yeah.

I rose, my hand on her front doorknob. "You said you love me? I don't know a lot about love, Marie. But the way you treat me, that's not love. I love you, anyway. But I'm not your punching bag either. So, if you can't let it go, I guess bring it."

"Bring it? Big tough wrestler. Nice black eye. Who kicked your ass?" A hint of a smile danced at the corners of her lips.

"It doesn't matter. Sometimes it's harder to lose on purpose. See you Monday morning." I slammed her door and ran back home.

My mom was at the house. She stood in front of the open fridge, staring at the casserole dishes inside it. She glanced at me but said nothing, showed not even the slightest surprise at my battered face.

"Three people came by and left those dishes earlier. Peter's mom left the lasagna. Ms., uh, Deppermann left the kugel. And, uh, I don't know the other woman's name, but she left some sort of chicken casserole."

She closed the fridge door. "I'll find out. Did you thank them?"

"Uh-huh." I wiped a gloss of sweat from my brow. "I was running. I need to take a shower. Is there anything I can do for you?"

Unexpectedly, her face crumpled, a tear trickled down her cheek, and she opened her arms. I slipped into her embrace, patting her back. Her frame felt so light in my arms like her flesh and bones were made of thin paper. It was a wonder the wind outside didn't blow her away. "Oh, Steven," she whispered, and then she wept into my shoulder. It was the only time I recall her being vulnerable, revealing to me that the machinations of her illogical mind, in the end, could not protect her from deep sorrow. Perhaps tomorrow—almost certainly tomorrow or even later today—she would snap back like a rubber band and return to her usual self, spouting the fabricated pseudo-religious reasons why my father, her husband, was destined to die. But for those few moments, she simply needed the comforting arms of her only son. "We'll be alright," she whispered. "It's you and me now, but we'll be alright. You'll see. God will provide."

I did not believe her.

1983

The Silent House

The year following my father's death, our house became even quieter than it had been since Cher died. During the last couple of years of my dad's life, his presence was a whisper; he would lie in repose on his sofa, rarely offering a comment. But after he died, the father-shaped indent in the sofa cushions vacuumed any happy sounds—laughter or casual conversation—from our house. Not that these sounds were all that common before he passed away. But once he was gone, our ranch home became a virtual crypt, its stagnant, silent air only occasionally punctuated by my mother's religious soliloquies.

I tried to make things easier for my mother. I helped her with tasks, sometimes driving to Winn Dixie on my own to buy us groceries. I cleaned the house more often, too, and I offered her a kind word when I could. I even accompanied her to church where everyone was always so nice to her, especially Pastor Gregg, whose wife had left him a year ago.

But my mother was a difficult person to love, at least for me. No matter what I did or said, she would bring the conversation back to her theories about why God had chosen us, specifically selected her, to endure the trials of Job. For her, suffering had become the point of life.

The clicking inside my shoulder, aggravated by my fight with Peter, proved my downfall. A week after I returned to practice in January, during a practice match in the wrestling room, I came down hard on my shoulder, and it separated. The orthopedist claimed it was an 'impressive' 2.5 separation, which apparently was quite bad. My promising junior season was over, and I spent several weeks in a brace-like sling that pressed the tip of my shoulder back into its socket. To dull the throbbing ache that radiated into my neck and jaw, I took a Percocet almost every day for two weeks, and my grades slipped some but not enough to matter.

I saw Marie every now and then, a reminder she wasn't finished with me. Sometimes when my mother was out, my sister would barge into the house and rustle around in her old bedroom. The timing of her intrusions was such that I wondered if she parked down the street and waited for our mother to leave before she rushed in to do whatever it was that she did in her bedroom. I wondered if, like Annie, my sister was using our home as a stash house and selling drugs. Like pot. Or cocaine.

That summer, I saved almost all the money I made working a new job at Movie City 11, and I bought a beat-up, 1978 Chevy Caprice. The theatre was a pleasant, lazy place to work, and I even let Peter and Joey into the movies for free twice. I gave my former friends a silent nod and allowed them to pass—without a ticket and without a word. I'm not sure why I did that. I suppose I felt a weird sense of loyalty to them because of our neighborhood ties.

On quiet weekday afternoons when the theatre manager left the building, Dave Wonka, some of the other ushers, and I would get high up in a projection room. Then we'd clean the theatres while stoned, which was harder than it looked; more than once I found myself bent and staring at an extra-large soda cup, wondering how long I'd been hunched in that position as a giggling Dave Wonka talked nonsense at me for the sole purpose of messing with my mind. All in all, except for changing the soda canister, working at Movie City 11 was a fun job, and I would have paid them to let me work there. We'd stand in the theatres and watch parts of the movies for free. I saw parts of *Risky Business* with Tom Cruise at least thirty-four times.

Two or three times a week, I lifted weights in the early morning at OP High, invading their weight room even though I wasn't a student there. Almost everyone at the local high school knew me from middle school, and nobody seemed to mind. The physical education teachers seemed happy that a state-caliber athlete was using their room, fawning over me when I showed up; the recognition felt, to be honest, like I was that football player, Wang, the guy who electrified the room by lifting tremendous amounts when Rob and I took summer gym as incoming freshmen. Two days a week, I drove myself to Broward Community College in Davie, to a club called Sea Anemone Wrestling, run by a coach named Ray Schlitz. Each time I pulled into the college parking lot, I fantasized that I would see Annie, who I imagined was attending school there and taking summer courses. I daydreamed that she'd see me and smile, and we'd hug and reminisce, and I'd ask her out. We'd eat dinner together, have a great time, and go back to her apartment and make love. Afterward, she'd tell me she loved me, and we'd make love again, even more passionately. But I never saw Annie, so of course, that fantasy never came true. Instead, that summer before senior year, I dated my ex-girlfriend Victoria on and off down in Hollywood when she wasn't busy seeing some other guy. One night, I called her to go out, and she informed me she was getting serious with one of my teammates. And that was that for Victoria. But I didn't care.

As the year progressed, I encountered Marie in our house less and less. I sensed that she had found somewhere else to hide her stash. Or maybe she had started invading our house while we weren't home. Perhaps she possessed a key to the front door and could come and go as she pleased. Who knew?

Toward the end of 1983, my mother started dating Pastor Gregg openly, so she was around less, too. On Saturdays, if my mother was home, I drove down to Sunrise Boulevard, to the public library, to get out of the house and to get away from her.

In November, I endured a painfully awkward family dinner at our house with Pastor Gregg and his adult son, also a pastor. Marie didn't show for the dinner, although she told my mom she would. My mother's face reddened at the dinner table when she realized my sister had purposefully stood her up.

In December, our wrestling season officially started, and out of the gate, I suffered an upset loss to Dave Luck, a young upstart from a cross-town rival, Mustang High, a bigger 4A school. I bounced back, though, and by the time the end-of-season district tournament rolled around, that first loss would be my only dual-meet loss.

Also in December, I was accepted into the University of Miami for the fall of 1984 on a full academic scholarship. My mother proclaimed, happily, that she could afford to send me there, but 'barely,' trying to spritz me with her guilt like holy water from a spray bottle. My father's life insurance policy had paid out a hefty amount, the reason she could afford to pay my room and board at a private college. I refused to feel guilty about going to Miami, though. I had so many other things weighing me down, and I'd worked hard for the scholarship.

In passing moments, I grew blue, but I did my best to shove my sadness way down inside. I promised myself I would not, like my father, allow myself to be dragged down by my guilt over Cher, my

191

loneliness at having lost Annie, or my inability to form a meaningful connection with my mother.

Yes, that was 1983, and it lacked any events worthy of mention, or at least it felt that way at the time.

It was a silent year in a silent house.

Outside our house, the gears of life rolled and rumbled, grinding us forward. Slowly. Seemingly, inconsequentially. Although looking back on it, even when it seemed like nothing was happening, something was happening.

But then the year ticked to 1984, and I ran into a fascinating young woman. A cute new-wave girl with pale skin, short dark hair, and a tight black T-shirt. She wore funky eyeglasses with thick square frames like those worn by the beautiful woman in the music video for "She Blinded Me with Science." My heart changed when I met her.

1984

Wrestling with the Enemy

New-wave Girl

Saturday, January 28, 1984

Broward Community College; Davie, Florida
District XVI High School Wrestling Tournament

Whoops. I was flying, flying, flying.

Moments before, I'd allowed my opponent to escape from under me, and I'd squared off and tied up with him. There were maybe five seconds remaining in the period, and I held a commanding lead, 10-2. So, I planned to tie up with him on my feet and stall for the remainder of the second period. I was in the clinch when something swatted my butt with a soft thud; I'd been hit by the rolled, taped towel the scoring table usually tossed onto the mat when they called time, a failsafe to ensure the referee knew the period had ended. The towel hit my backside, the referee's whistle shrieked, and I relaxed. As my body slackened, my opponent, desperate for points, cinched my head and arm within both his arms and corkscrewed me over his hip in a headlock with no time on the clock. I went sailing into the air, and as I hit the mat, I instinctively spun through his throw. His hips were too

196

high, and I rolled him to his back, but the ref was already on top of us, his whistle shrieking as he wrenched us apart, shouting, "No points! Period was over! Caution, red!" Warning my opponent for the late move.

My bulldog of a coach yelled at me from his corner, something about not letting up, not relaxing. Blah, blah. Okay, okay. I heard him, but I was focused on the ref, who was now embroiled in a heated conversation at the edge of the mat with the girl who held the taped-up towel. The ref was explaining to the girl, maybe not so nicely, that she couldn't carry her timer clock onto the mat *or* touch the wrestlers with the towel. He was instructing her that as the timer ticked to zero, she should have thrown the towel where he could see it or, failing that, she should have walked onto the mat and swatted *him* on the arm with the towel. The girl, all five feet and four inches of her, faced him defiantly, arms folded across her chest, towel dangling from one hand. She wore hi-cut blue jean shorts and a tight, tucked-in black T-shirt bearing a photo of the new-wave musical group *Flock of Seagulls*. Her skin looked like she'd lost her summer tan during the mild winter. Her hair, dyed jet-black, was styled in a short, crop cut. Reddish-brown thick-framed glasses completed her funky, new-wave look.

There was something familiar about the way she stood, squaring off with the ref, but as I considered this, my coach's booming voice drew my focus from her and the referee. "Stevie! Stevie!" My hard-faced coach, in fact, all three-hundred pounds of him, caught my attention. "Put this match away, Stevie. Quit fooling around with this guy." This was a semi-finals match, and I hadn't been fooling around, but okay, maybe I could end it. I nodded at him, thinking that the sooner the match ended, the sooner I'd be able to get a close-up look at the fascinating girl keeping time.

I started the last period on top, worked my favorite pinning combination, and, as my coach requested, ended the match quickly. My coach nodded and clapped, like 'much better, much better.' I shook the opposing coach's hand. Then I shook my own coach's hand, and he swatted my butt as I headed toward the scorer's table, the ceremoniousness butt slapping feeling sort of stupid. I walked up to the scorer's table to confirm my win and to sign and circle my bout sheet...and to check out the timer girl. I wiped the sweat from my cheeks with my forearm, and I snuck a glance at the new-wave girl working the clock. She caught me looking. "Nice job, Steven. You sure get sweaty out there, don't you?"

That voice. What? I focused on her symmetrical face. Really looked at her.

The world stood still. Time halted.

I leaned toward her, my hands gripping the edge of the wooden table. It couldn't be. The baby fat in her once chubbier cheeks had vanished. Her skin was less tanned. Her dirty-blonde hair, which once had waterfalled around her shoulders, had been replaced by this dark, punk, Pat Benatar hairdo. The slight almond shape of her light brown eyes was hidden behind her thick, quirky frames.

But it was her.

"Annie?"

"Lynn," she replied with a wink and a sly smile as the next two wrestlers checked in with the scorer beside her.

"Jacobs!" the referee yelled, waving me away. "We're trying to start the next match, Jacobs. Quit looking for a date and get out from in front of my timekeeper."

This referee, with his lightbulb-shaped head, was such a dick.

I turned my attention back to Annie, and I pointed at the stands. "When you get done working this table, there's an hour break before the finals. I'm sitting over there at the top. My team is in the dark green and white sweatsuits."

"I know. Same color as your singlet." She pointed at my chest and shot me a dubious look.

"Oh, yeah. Right."

"Jacobs! Move!" the ref yelled.

"See you over there," she said, and my heart swelled. Annie was here. She looked like she'd been rolled through an MTV-machine, but it was Annie. Lynn? Analynn LeFevre. My friend. And she said she would come over to the stands to speak with me.

About thirty minutes later, Chris and I lounged way up in the highest bleacher, well above our teammates. Each of us, along with four other wrestlers from my team, had won our way into the district finals. "What's up with you and that timer girl?" he asked. "I was right behind Coach during your match when she hit your butt with the towel. Then you were talking to her, and the ref was pissed."

"So?"

"So. She's nice looking. Really hot body in that tight T-shirt. But you don't usually go for the new-wave girls."

Hot body? I smiled to myself, recalling the day several years ago when sixteen-year-old Annie had flashed me and surlily asked my opinion. I'd offered her a restrained response—they're fine—even though she had blown my young mind.

"Well, there's more to a girl than her body," I replied, a trace of irritation in my voice. This was my good friend, Analynn, not a walking pair of tits.

He shot me a look that said, 'duh,' and then he said, "Duh," as he glanced toward the bottom of the bleachers, where his girlfriend, Jackie, and my ex-girlfriend from sophomore year, Rosie, sat talking to Chris's parents.

"Mmm," I answered. "Maybe you should stop checking out other girls."

"Oh, yeah? Ya' think? Hey, look at that, she's coming up here. So, do you know this girl from somewhere?"

"Yeah, I know her." I gulped. Here she was, standing in front of us, only one bleacher-step down, hands on her hips. I studied her face. It was obviously Annie, but at a glance, you would never know.

"It's nice that you admit to knowing me, Steven." She chuckled dryly and sat beside me, her bare thigh pressing against my dark green sweatpants. "I'm Lynn," she introduced herself to Chris.

"I'm Chris."

"I know who you are. I came here with my apartment mate, Mary, because her brother wrestles for Miramar. They roped me into working a table all day," she explained. "The moment we walked in here, Mary pointed you out. She's like, that guy is the best in Florida. I think she's a little bit in love with you." She laughed and jutted her chin at a blonde-haired timekeeper who was working the last semi-final match of the day, a heavyweight match. "I could introduce you."

"Nah. Sorry," Chris replied. "Not gonna happen."

"I told you Chris had a girlfriend. Jackie," I explained to her.

"Oh, yeah. Jackie." She eyed my forehead. "You look good, Steven. A little sweaty, and you should get that scratch looked at." For a moment, I thought she might reach out and trace her fingertip across the scratch on my forehead, a cut I'd somehow gotten during my first match of the day. The memory of Annie cleaning my lip the last time I saw her, our last kiss, flashed into my brain.

"So, how do you guys know each other?" Chris asked.

"This is Annie," I explained to him.

"Ohhh. This is *your* Annie?"

"Your Annie?" Her brows lowered. "Am I yours, Steven?"

200

Chris backpedaled for me. "No, it's just that Steve talked about you all the time. That's all. But he said you were a dirty blonde."

She smirked. "I am a blonde. And sometimes I'm dirty. But this is a dye job in case it's not obvious."

"You got a little thinner, too." I followed this immediately with, "But you look good. You look great."

She placed her hand on my knee as if to calm me down. "How are you, Stevie?"

"I–I'm okay. After my dad died—"

"What? Oh, my God!" Her eyes widened. "Your dad passed? I'm so sorry."

She didn't know. "I never got a chance to tell you. That night when Peter and me scrapped at your house, my dad died the day before. He had a massive heart attack. A lot of stuff happened, and then you were gone. I should have told you." I blinked. Tears welled in my eyes quite unexpectedly. Chris wouldn't care if I cried, but still, I was embarrassed. I wasn't tearing up because my father had died, but because Analynn never said goodbye to me. And now, here she was. And it was overwhelming.

She squeezed my knee. "I'm sorry, Steven. For your dad. For everything. I had to leave it all behind quickly. I mailed Danny some money and a letter telling him I couldn't afford to keep the house anymore. I'm sure he and his boss didn't care much that I bolted. The Mexicans sure didn't care about me—I bet I was easily replaced. But it was safer if I left the scene quickly."

"Mexicans?" Chris asked, but she ignored him. I'd never told him she dealt pot.

"What are you doing now?" I asked her.

"I found a roommate and moved to Davie. I work in a small restaurant out here waiting tables. I started school at BCC last semester. It's going well."

"I'm happy for you. What are you studying?"

"Business. I'm thinking about transferring up to Gainesville after two years. I've got money from selling my house, and my grades are good."

"That's awesome."

"Where are you going next year?"

"University of Miami."

"La de da." She laughed. "Private college."

I shrugged. "They're paying my way. You look good...Lynn. I like your hair." Her hairstyle and glasses were stylish, sexy. Then again, it was Annie, and she always looked good.

"I'm so sorry about your dad, Steven. If I'd known, I would have snuck back to see you. Really, I'm sorry. I didn't have a clue."

For the first time since she'd started speaking to me, it clicked that somebody had worked with Analynn on her elocution. Her southern accent was concealed, and she spoke with a more stilted, neutral-sounding brand of English, using proper grammar and more formal diction. Or maybe she'd worked on her accent herself. Was she merely imitating the speech patterns of those around her now, her college classmates and professors? I wanted to tell her that she sounded different, good, but I thought twice about saying something like that; it would have been rude. Analynn LeFevre had transformed herself, quite intentionally, from redneck Annie to new-wave Lynn. She had become who she wanted to become. And there was nothing wrong—and everything right—with that. No matter who she was, the splendor at Analynn's core shined above all else. Her outward appearance didn't matter much to me.

"It's okay. I understand why you had to go. It's really, really good to see you…Lynn." I swallowed hard and took a chance, a leap. "We should go to a movie or dinner sometime."

She exhaled hard. "I–I can't Steven. Sorry."

"Ouch," breathed Chris, studying his wrestling shoes.

My heart sank. I may just as well have lost my finals match. "Okay," I replied, a question wrapped up in my one-word response: Why not?

Instead of answering, or maybe as part of her answer, she leaned in and hugged me. Her short, dark hair smelled like apples. The same as ever. Like it did when she presented twelve-year-old me with my first kiss in 1978. Like it did in 1982 when we came one interrupting phone call away from making love. She rubbed small circles on my back and spoke into my ear. "It wasn't meant to be. I had my own problems. I had to leave quick, and I didn't want to put you through that. I still don't want to hurt you. I love you," she whispered, her breath hot in my ear. "I heard you tell me you love me before I left. And I did love you. I love you, Steven. But I can't. I just can't, honey." She pulled out of our embrace, and her eyes were glistening. She wiped at them with her index finger. "I'm up here in Davie. You're going down to Miami. Maybe someday we'll get together, though, huh?" she said loudly enough that Chris could hear, allowing me to save face, although I didn't need to do that with my good friend.

'Someday' meant never, and I knew that. But she'd already given me what I needed. She'd said the words. She loved me once. And I believed her.

"Uh oh, you got on the girls' radar," Chris muttered, then laughed nervously as he tracked Jackie and Rosie tromping up the bleacher steps toward us.

Rosie wore a look on her face like I'd cheated on her or something even though she and I hadn't dated in almost two years. Jackie offered us a sweet smile, showing most of her teeth and, it seemed, thinly veiling the jealousy brewing inside her.

Analynn rose. As she stood, a hole spread inside my chest, a chasm churning with dismal, dark gray clouds. "Steven, I'm gonna go. It was good meeting you, Chris. Good luck in the finals. Hey, is your mom around, Steven?"

"Yeah, she's down there with the other parents." I pointed down at my mother.

"Good. Marie's not here?"

"No."

"Hey, Steven…"

"Yeah?"

"Watch out for Marie. Really, watch out for her. She's the type of person who doesn't let stuff go."

"I know."

"What?" Chris mumbled. I hadn't told him much about my ongoing silent battle with my sister.

"I've got an ace in the hole when it comes to Marie." I'd kept the note my father wrote tucked away.

"Okay. Still, be careful. Watch yourself."

"I will. Can I have your number, Lynn?"

She looked at me like I was a small child asking for dessert before dinner. "I love you, Steven. Have a happy life." With that, she left.

Did she really say that to me, spin, and hop down the bleacher steps, sidling past Jackie and Rosie with a sweet smile? Yes. Yes, she did.

"You should go after her," mumbled Chris.

My eyes followed her down the bleacher steps. "No. I don't think so. It's complicated."

"Who was that?" Rosie asked, trying to sound like she was posing an innocent question and not assuming a defensive posture against an interloper.

"Steve's in love with her," Chris shot back. "And she loves him. But it's not meant to be."

Thank you, Chris, master of the obvious. Shpresa must have woken from her slumber under the gym bleachers.

I bit the inside of my bottom lip. "She's an old friend."

"Old is right. She looks older than us," Jackie commented.

"She's nineteen. She'll be twenty this Saint Patrick's Day."

"That's a day after your birthday." Rosie sat beside me. Wait, Rosie remembered my birthday?

"Yeah."

"What did she want?" Jackie asked.

"I think she wanted to warn me."

"About your finals match."

"No. About something else."

Maybe she was put here today to give you that warning. Last year was a sleepy year. Most mornings you don't wake up and think about Marie. But maybe you should.

Shpresa, my mom is off with Pastor Gregg half the time. I don't do drugs. I've got my father's real letter, where he said he knew the drugs were Marie's, in case it ever comes to that. I'm going to be eighteen in a couple of months. My sister's going to have a hard time getting me in trouble.

Is she? Then why the warning from a good friend? Why would Analynn bring that up?

The three of them—Chris, Jackie, and Rosie—were staring at me. Waiting for me to tell them what the strange, new-wave girl's warning was all about. "It was nothing. Who are you wrestling in the finals?" I asked Chris. I knew who Chris's finals' opponent would be, but I wanted to change the subject. I watched Analynn stroll across the gym floor, meet up with her apartment mate, Mary, and head toward the gym door. She walked through the door without glancing up at me. As she went away, the song "Karma Chameleon" by Boy George played low on the gym speakers.

Sometimes, when you leave somebody or they leave you, a tingle wraps its way around your body, and you're blanketed by an almost spiritual presence, which informs you that, yes, you will never see that person again. God, the gods, or whoever, remind you that person was important to you, and in your special way you loved them, and they loved you, but that you reached the end of things with them. That feeling enveloped me as Analynn's trail leg disappeared out the gym door. I believed I'd never see her again. And I was right in that feeling. That day was the end of things for her and me.

There isn't much more to say at this point about Analynn LeFevre. She was my first love, but this is obviously not a love story.

Fishing

Saturday, February 18, 1984

The weekend after the wrestling season ended, all I wanted to do was rest, and I planned to do just that. Then, late Saturday morning, I got the strangest, most irritating phone call.

My mother and Pastor Gregg were out somewhere. Maybe they were at a religious event, or maybe they were drinking Bloody Marys down at *Shooters* on the Intercoastal. Anyone's guess was as good as mine. My mom had informed me they were going to be gone all day and all night. They were planning to go to dinner and a movie later, and she said I shouldn't worry if she came home late, like eleven or twelve.

I lay watching MTV on the family room sofa, crashed in my dad's old spot. The video for "What Is Love" by Howard Jones was playing when the kitchen phone rang. I thought maybe Chris was calling because he was planning to come over to my house that night.

"Hello, uh, Jacobs' residence."

"Yes, may I please speak with Linnea Jacobs?" It was a young woman's voice. Sharp. Familiar. Why did her tone, so formal, send a small chill down my spine?

"She's not here. May I take a message?"

"Is," papers shuffled on the other end of the line, "Is your father there? I can't seem to find his name. Mr. Jacobs."

"I'm sorry, he passed away about a year ago."

"Oh. My sympathies. My name is Rebeccah Childs."

The short hairs on my arms prickled to attention, and my mouth went dry. That's where I knew that voice. Her. An image popped into my head of a massive alligator, golden eyes aglow, lying silent in the grassy swamp at the edge of the Everglades. Waiting.

Monster.

She continued. "I'm the Head of Client Services and Rejuvenation at Straight and Narrow Teen and Young Adult Rest and Rehabilitation Center." A couple of silent beats stretched across the line. "Formerly known as The Sprout."

She paused again like she was waiting for me to say something. All I could think of to say after swallowing hard was, "Yes." I wasn't sure to what I was agreeing—that The Sprout's new name sucked?

"We like to check up on our former residents. See how they're doing. With whom am I speaking?"

Don't tell her your real name. Shpresa poked her head up.

"I'm Sam. Sam Jacobs. Linnea's son."

"Yes. I don't know why that's not noted here. We have Maria Jacobs listed as a sister. File mix up I suppose. Well, I'll note it here that you're her brother. Cher Jacobs is your sister, too, then?"

Maria? Cher Jacobs? Cher's last name was Rankin. These people hadn't even recorded Cher's name or familial relationships properly. Something cold and hard blossomed in my chest. A stone. An angry stone. Not a rock radiating white-hot rage. No, a small, smooth, hard stone, freezing to the touch. The anger contained by this stone in my heart threatened to crack and spread across my skin like the frost I'd once seen on my father's car windshield when I was ten and it snowed in South Florida. At that instant, I could have turned into an ice monster.

"Yes. Cher is my sister." I lied twice. "Maria is my sister, too."

"Well, we're checking to see how some of our residents are getting along. How is your sister, Cher?"

She kept saying, 'well.' "Cher's doing really good. She's up at Boston College. Second year, Biology major. Pre-med."

These people didn't even know what happened to Cher. They didn't even know what they did to her, what became of her. They didn't know, and they didn't care.

"Oh, wow. Very nice school. Catholic college." She said 'Catholic' with a small note of disdain.

"Yes, she's doing fine."

"Good," she said brusquely, not sounding overly happy at the news. "Good to hear."

I wondered if she would ask for Cher's phone number. What would I do if she did?

But she didn't.

"Well, I'll be going then." She paused. "How are you doing, Samuel?"

A memory surfaced of this woman probing my brain, my soul, in her tiny wood-paneled office outside of the airplane hangar. Searching for a weakness, a crack in my facade. Trying to snap me up in her alligator jaws and carry me to her master, Howel Carnavale.

I gritted my teeth at the memory of her questioning me. Why was I gritting my teeth?

Give her nothing.

Yes, I'll give her nothing, Shpresa.

"Good. I'm good. I'm going to Florida State in the fall. You know, uh, keeping it on the straight and narrow." Ugh, why did I say that?

Wow. Do not ever go into comedy.

The woman ignored my bad joke. "Tell Linnea we said hello, and we're so glad everything worked out with Cher, would you please?"

"Uh, yes. Sure."

"God bless, Samuel. See you later."

The line clicked. See me later?

I examined the handset. What had just happened?

She is fishing for druggies. Your parents kept quiet about what happened to Cher, so it's not surprising Cher's death wasn't on their radar. Their residency numbers are down, and she's doing outreach, searching for troubled souls who backslid. Looking for a quick cash infusion to their business. Because that's what it is for them mostly. A business.

Ohhh, she was hoping Cher had gone back to doing drugs.

Yes. The more drugs, the better. So, she could console your mother. Speak with her about options. But she didn't know that Cher died. She didn't know much of anything, really. With these people, it's on to the next one.

She didn't even know Cher killed herself. And she didn't care. She was like, oh, your dad died, so sorry. Can I get Cher back into The Sprout, which we're calling blah-blah-blah now? No? How are you, young man? Do you do drugs?

Exactly. And, as you can see, Rebeccah is still there.

Marie said she left.

Marie lied. Marie lies.

The stone in my chest grew from cold to warm to molten-lava hot.

"Those fuckers," I spat as the video for "Somebody's Watching Me" by Rockwell played on our boxy television. "Those fuckers."

My friend Chris was the type of person who could size up how somebody was feeling in a single glance. Perspicacious was the word for that, I think, or, more specifically, empathic, attuned to others' feelings. He sensed my troubled state from the moment I opened my front door.

"Thanks for driving up here," I said, trying to mask the anxiousness that had latched onto my shoulders since I'd spoken with Rebeccah Childs earlier in the day. "What's Jackie doing tonight?"

"She's with Rosie and Ginny for a girls' night out. Hey, man, what's wrong with you?"

I chuckled. As if any of the thoughts or feelings rumbling around my brain were amusing. "Is it that obvious?" I opened the slider to the patio, and we entered the tiny concrete enclosure above the manmade lake behind my house. He and I dropped into wrought-iron chairs at the wrought-iron table crammed into the small space. The sun had set, and bright stars twinkled above us.

"You've got on a face, man." He tossed me a beer can, which he produced from the brown paper bag in his lap. "Here, drink one of these first. If you're in a bad mood and smoke the stuff I brought, you might get paranoid. You need to chill first." He popped the top on his beer and took a sip.

I opened my beer and drank, too. The beer was warm and bitter in my mouth, and it went down hard. I took another deep swig, which slid down my throat easier. I extended my beer can toward him for a toast. "Here's to you. You did it. Congrats." We clinked beer cans and drank. Chris had reached his goal of winning a 3A state championship. He'd won in overtime on a last-second takedown. In contrast, I'd been upset in the state quarterfinals. The way tournaments worked in Florida at the time, to move into the consolation bracket and wrestle for third or fourth place, the person who beat you needed to reach the finals match. The wrestler who beat me in the quarterfinals was winning his semi-final match handily before he was stunningly pinned in the last few seconds. I was watching his match and warming up to wrestle in the first consolation round, but once he lost, that was that. I was out of the tournament, and my high school wrestling career was over. But I never really wanted to place in the state tournament anyway. My goal merely had been to qualify for the tournament itself and take the trip to Pinellas Park on Florida's west coast. What you want, what you strive for, makes all the difference. Chris had one burning goal, to win a championship, and his desire to go all the way proved to be an advantage I didn't possess.

"We're on to the next thing, bud. I'm up to Michigan. You to Miami." He took another drink, and I mimicked him, taking a bigger drink. He and Jackie planned to attend a small DIII school in Michigan, our high school wrestling coach's college. Chris had been given a partial scholarship to wrestle there. "You're going to do great in Miami. There's no wrestling, but the football is good," he said, lighting a joint, puffing on it, and handing it to me. The pot's rich, skunky odor filled the patio. He exhaled like a dragon, and the smoke drifted into the clear, cool, South Florida night sky.

I pinched the joint, took a hit. Inhaled. I held the smoke in my lungs for a few seconds like my friend Peter had taught me when we smoked the joint that I'd pilfered from my sister so many years ago. I exhaled. Then I repeated the process, inhaling, holding, and exhaling. Chris was right, the beer had relaxed me, and as the pot took effect, my limbs melted into the metal of the chair. I handed him the joint. "Good shit, man."

We both laughed.

We drank another beer. We smoked.

My brain grew soft around the edges, my head wrapped in cotton gauze. Time warped. We sat outside, drinking and smoking and chatting on my small patio for thirty minutes. One hour? Two hours? My will softened, my mind homing in on one thing—one person: Annie. I opened my mouth to say something about wrestling to Chris, and instead, her name tumbled out. I explained to my best friend what Analynn LeFevre really meant to me. Like a sliced-open shark, I spilled my innards onto the patio, revealing all the items I had accidentally ingested on the seemingly never-ending foray through the deep dark ocean of my teen years: a ping pong paddle with red rubber peeling around the edges, a yellow tank top clutched to Annie's chest, a small pile of marijuana dotted with pocket lint, a baggie of pot and Quaaludes, a movie theatre ticket to see *Fast Times*, a GED exam study guide on a cable-spool coffee table, and a cool alcohol wipe brushing my lip. I told Chris how close Annie and I became when I helped her study for the GED. How we kissed. That we never slept together, but it didn't matter. How we were in love with each other once but did nothing about it. She told me she loved me, but she didn't think she was right for me. And that was that.

Chris was normally a good listener, but I had a hard time discerning if he was processing my words, or if he was staring at me simply because he was stoned. He stubbed out the joint, now a small burnt roach, under his sneaker on the cement patio. "You really dig her. I don't blame you. She's smoking hot, and she seemed really cool."

Was that all he had taken away from what I just told him? That I was in love with Annie because she was attractive? Or cool? "There's more to life than being cool."

"She had a little southern accent, huh?" he questioned, turning to a different topic. "Like a twang or something."

"Who, Annie?"

"Yeah, Analynn, right? Lynn."

"Annie. Did you notice she had an accent? Maybe you did because I told you once I was hanging out with a girl with a southern accent. It seemed like she worked hard over the last year to get rid of it."

"Yeah, she was hiding it, but it came through a little. I could tell."

"What are you trying to say?" My voice quavered. Was he saying Annie and I weren't right because she was a southerner at heart? From a different class? What did he know?

"Nothing. I'm just saying, is all. Hey, what were you so upset about when I showed up tonight? Not her, right?" He changed the topic effortlessly, once again. "Also, I'm hungry. You got any chips?"

Rebeccah's call from earlier in the day flashed into my head, killing my buzz. I opened my mouth to answer him, to tell him about the bogeywoman, at the same time the patio sliding door shuddered open.

Look who was standing in my family room. Oh, shit.

Once a Druggie, always a Druggie

I blinked furiously, hoping that doing so would set my reeling mind straight, but the pulsing in my temples continued. I squeezed my eyes shut and pressed two fingers on each side of my head.

Yeah, that's not going to help, Steven. Just say hello to her.

"Hey, Marie. What are you doing here?"

Marie assessed us from the family room before she stepped down onto the patio. She wore a mini-skirt and a satiny purple blouse, her luxurious blonde hair perfectly waved and teased up in the front. She sniffed. "Look at you, getting high, little bro."

"Hey. This is my good friend from school, Chris. Chris, this is my sister, Marie."

"I know Chris. We met when I came to your match that one time in tenth grade."

Marie had come to my first varsity wrestling match when I was a sophomore. I'd been dropped on my head by an overly aggressive wrestler, and she never came back to another match. She said she could not bear to watch me get hurt. Imagine that.

"Hey," Chris said sheepishly.

215

"What are you doing here?" I repeated.

She shrugged. "What am I ever doing here?"

"I know you're hiding drugs in the house," I blurted.

She tsk'd.

"Can I have some?" Chris asked. A weak joke.

"Maybe I am stashing my stuff here. Maybe I'm grabbing some alone time in my old room." She walked toward me, her heels clicking on the cement. She poked my shoulder. "Maybe I'm messing with your head, stoner."

"Stop." I swatted her hand away.

"You want to smoke a joint with us?" Chris asked her. He was trying to be friendly, but I hoped she would say no. There was no way I could smoke another joint and make it off the patio on my own two feet.

"No, thanks. I'm going out to a club later."

"With Rick?"

"No, a girlfriend from Summers on the Beach where I bartend."

"Hmm."

She waved her index fingers around the patio. "You better hope Mom doesn't come home early and walk out here. It smells like Cheech and Chong on this patio."

"Mom's not coming home until late. She's out to dinner and a movie with Pastor Gregg."

Marie scoffed. "Pastor Gregg. Always staring at my boobs in church. As if." She laughed dryly. "I think you should go inside the house, now, Steven. You never know when Mom's going to come home early."

The sound of the front door shutting inside the house came through the open sliding glass door.

My throat constricted, and my palms grew sweaty. "What did you do, Marie?" I whispered. "What did you do?"

Chris leaped up, grabbed the empty beer cans, and shoved them into the paper bag. He hopped over the low patio wall, presumably stashing the bag on the other side, on the hill that dropped several feet to the man-made lake. Chris climbed back over the patio wall a second before my mother appeared in the rectangle of light created by the open sliding door.

"Ms. Jacobs," Chris said as he dropped into his chair. "You have a lovely lake back here."

Lovely lake?

"Christopher," my mom greeted him icily by his full first name, and she raised her nose into the air and sniffed. Her brows lowered, and her lips puckered.

"I *told* you," my sister claimed triumphantly. "See?"

"Chris, you should go home." My mom pointed through the slider door, directing him into the family room.

"Uh, okay. See you, man." Chris shot me a worried look, stood, and hopped over the patio wall again. "I'll just go around the house." He disappeared around the corner of our house. "Call me, Steve," his voice rang from the side of the house.

I didn't answer him. I was too busy swallowing the bile that had peeked its way up my throat from my roiling stomach. I closed my eyes to calm myself. The last thing I needed right now was to throw up in front of my mother.

My mother sat in the chair Chris left empty. She clasped her hands on the tabletop. "What were you doing out here, Steven? And don't lie to me."

"Nothing."

"Nothing? It smells like burnt marijuana back here, Steven."

How would she know?

"How would you know?"

"Steven, do not take that insolent tone with me." She sighed. "You had it all, Steven. But I can't let drugs take you the way they took Cynthia's daughter." Pause. "The way they took Cher."

My jaw clenched. "Are you fucking kidding me?"

My mother's head snapped back, her mouth dropped open, and she grabbed at the cross on her chest. She shook her head. "This is how it starts with the abusive language. Steven, tomorrow I am going to Straight and Narrow and pick up forms to sign. You'll be going there for the spring. You can graduate high school next year when you're clean."

"I'm as clean as I need to be, and I'm not going anywhere." My eyes burned. But I would not cry. I blinked. I would not cry for her.

"Yes, you are going there because I say you are."

"I'm eighteen next month. And you don't have any evidence I did anything illegal. You can't threaten me with jail. You can't send me anywhere."

"She can," said Marie, who observed us with her arms folded across her chest. "Because there's proof."

My mother pursed her lips again, rose from the patio table, and marched into the house. "We'll see what I can do," she called back as I scurried after her into the house and down hallway, my heart pounding. Where was she going and why? She strode to my bedroom, its door wide. Did I leave my door open? I didn't think so. My twin mattress hung slightly askew on the box spring. She lifted the mattress corner and pulled out a small baggie the size of a large pencil eraser. It was filled with white powder. She spun, her eyes skewering me on their pointy tips. "You want evidence? This is evidence." She thrust the baggie at me.

"What the hell is that?" I swiped at it, but she yanked it out of my reach.

"I told you, Mother." Marie had followed us down the hall. My sister's voice was maddeningly low and even. "Once a druggie, always a druggie. Half of Cher's stash was his. And now you know."

My cheeks grew red hot, the injustice of it all boiling through my veins like molten copper, glowing bright yellow and smelling like angry blood. "What a fucking liar you are, Marie!" I yelled, edging toward my sister. She stepped back, and I took another step forward, getting into her face. "You're a dirty liar, and you better tell Mom the truth. You told her once that the drugs Dad found were yours. Admit it!"

My mother thrust a hand between us, nearly slapping me in the chest. "Don't you dare touch her, Steven, or I will call the police. I don't feel safe around you."

My shoulders slumped, and I stepped back from Marie. "That's not my coke, Mom. You've got to believe me."

My sister smiled slyly. "How do you know it's coke?"

"Whatever it is."

The letter. Show your mom the real letter your dad wrote.

I edged past Marie, got on my belly, and pulled the shoebox from far underneath my bed. "Let me show you the truth," I said with my back to them. "I've got a letter."

"He might have a gun!" Marie shouted. My mother shrieked, and my bedroom door slammed behind me. Footsteps thump-thump-thumped toward the other side of the house.

It's like your sister is a hypnotist. She says something is true, and it magically becomes true in your mother's head.

You're just figuring that out, Shpresa?

My mother thought I had a gun? Honestly? I couldn't be bothered with the nonsense outside my bedroom door; I was too busy pulling crepe paper out of the shoe box, searching for the folded, wrinkled truth. But nothing was there.

My. Father's. Letter. Was. Gone.

My legs quivered, and I dropped to my knees on my bedroom carpet. My stomach twisted once again, and a shadow, dark and oily, blossomed up from my stomach to my chest to my head. I grabbed the small plastic wastebasket beside my bed and heaved into it, spewing liquid horror, a sour yellowish-brown stew, from my gut.

She got you. Well, Annie warned you. I warned you. I suppose it won't be so bad. You can fake it 'til you make it...make it out of rehab. If you're forced to return to high school next year, maybe you can wrestle another season.

How could this happen? How could Marie do this to me? It's so unfair.

I sat on my bed, head in my hands. Tears squeaked from my burning eyes and streamed down my cheeks.

You'll be okay.

I want to move on, Shpresa. I need to move on.

The truth seared the inside of my chest, branding itself on my heart: *Shpresa, I need to get out of this house.*

You'll be okay.

Will I?

I rose from my bed and staggered out of my room in search of my mother and Marie. There was nobody in the house. My mother had left a note on the kitchen table that she was sleeping on Gregg's couch. She wrote that she didn't feel safe in the house with me, but she didn't want to call the police. She hoped I would confess about the cocaine, which she had flushed, and accept that I needed help. She told me she loved me. Of that I had no doubt. A mother's love could wrap you in chains, smother, and suffocate you as easily as it could caress you with a gentle hand.

I lay on my bed and stared at the dark ceiling for most of the rest of the night. I didn't even try to fall asleep.

I was screwed. Almost four years after I'd stolen an eighth of an ounce of pot and twenty dollars from Marie to pay back Annie, my sister had taken her revenge on me. She told me she would get me back. And she did.

At about three in the morning, I submitted to slumber. I dreamed I was awake, staring at the ceiling.

The Bad Gal

Sunday, February 19, 1984

I woke late the next day, my mouth dry and a dull ache throbbing between my eyes. In the hall bathroom, I cupped my hand under the sink faucet, gathering enough water to suck down a couple of Tylenol. After using the toilet, I stumbled to the kitchen. My mom sat at the kitchen table, glasses at the tip of her nose, filling in paperwork. "I'd like you to sign these papers," she muttered as she scanned one of the pages.

This was really happening. My life was over.

"I didn't do anything wrong, and I'm not signing anything. Marie planted that baggie of whatever, and that's all." I banged around the kitchen, childishly making noise while I gathered ingredients to make fried eggs and toast. "You want breakfast?" I asked her. My stomach was still raw, and I wasn't sure if I could eat anything, but I wasn't about to give her the satisfaction of knowing how sick I felt. "And I do not have a gun," I proclaimed randomly. "That's stupid."

"Marie said you probably didn't." She shuffled the papers, appraising a new sheet.

222

"Whatever Marie says goes," I snapped back. I repeated my question, hard: "Do you want me to make you some breakfast?"

"No. I want you to get well," she whispered. Her face had gone deathly pale, and she'd stopped writing on the forms. She froze, gazing at her own hands. She looked so lost and scared that for a moment, I felt sorry for her. She really had no clue about anything. That thought sparked a flame of irritation in my chest, and soon I was banging around making breakfast again. Irate once more.

"I spoke with Ms. Childs this morning, and—"

"Let me tell you something about Rebeccah Childs." I interrupted her, my attention on the frying pan on the stove. "That woman called yesterday, and she didn't even know Cher died. She's awful."

"She admitted there was a mix-up with Cher's file, and she apologized for that. She said she spoke with you yesterday. She also said you didn't inform her about Cher, and that you called yourself Sam. *Sam?* Lies, Steven." Her eyes welled with tears. "She explained to me that druggies can't help but tell lies. The lying becomes a part of you, becomes woven into your fabric. And that's why you need someone to help you remove the evil that's knitted itself into your soul."

"I didn't call myself Sam," I lied, flipping the fried eggs. "She's wrong about that."

My mom sighed. "When are you going to stop lying, Steven? This is why I can't let things go on like this. You're all I've got now."

I blew out a hot stream of air. "I'm an honors student. I got a full academic scholarship to college. I went to the state wrestling tournament. What more do you want from me? What more could I do?" My voice rose with each sentence, my volume out of control. I was coming in hot. And getting hotter. My neck warmed as I scraped the eggs onto a plate. I pictured myself spinning away from the stove on the back wall, hurling the frying pan across the kitchen and family room, and shattering the sliding glass doors. As if by taking such drastic action, the truth would somehow pierce her thick skull. I closed my eyes and breathed. That was not the way.

Don't come in hot. Be cool.

Okay. Okay. Okay. Cool.

Breathe. Breathe.

Okay, Shpresa, I'm breathing.

"What do you want from me, Mom?" I asked again in a lower voice.

"I want you to not do drugs, Steven. I want you to stop lying."

A thought flashed into my head. "You didn't tell Chris's—"

"I spoke with his mother. I let her know I thought you two were smoking marijuana on our patio. She thanked me. She said she would take care of it."

I didn't think Chris's mom would do anything, really. She wore a golden cross around her neck, the same as my mom did, and yet the Halligan's tiny house in Hollywood smelled of simmering tomato sauce and pragmatic sensibility.

"What, you're not going to make sure Chris gets put into The Sprout?"

"Chris Halligan is not my son. And it's called the Straight and Narrow now."

"You want the truth, Mom?" I sat across from her at the table with my plate of toast and eggs.

"Yes. I would very much like the truth."

"The truth is," I tried to squelch the quiver in my voice, "That the pot Dad found in Marie's room was mostly Marie's. The pills were all hers. I don't know why you couldn't see that. The stuff was in her room. And the truth is, I haven't done drugs for years. I don't do drugs. I might drink a beer or two when I'm with my wrestling friends. We all do. Everyone drinks, and I'll be legal to drink next month anyway. But that cocaine…whatever it was under my bed last night, that stuff was *not* mine. Marie put that there. And the truth is that Dad knew the stash he found was Marie's. But he let Cher take the blame. He wrote a note about it while he was waiting for the ambulance. I found his note, and I rewrote it because I didn't want Marie to get in trouble. I forged his handwriting, but I left out the parts where he admitted he knew the drugs were Marie's. I took his real note and hid it in a shoebox. It's been under my bed for safe keeping this whole time, but Marie took it, maybe when she planted the coke. She's been snooping around, and she took it."

My mom shook her head dubiously. "Oh, Steven. Steven, please." She did not believe a word. "Why would your sister plant cocaine in your room?"

I sighed. I was going into the rehab, there was no doubt about that. I might as well tell her the entire truth. Not that she would believe it. "So, there's more to the story. The day before Dad found the pot, I was at my friend Annie's house."

Her face pinched at the mention of Annie. "That girl."

"Yes, that girl. That *girl* is in college now. Anyway, her grandma was senile, and Annie kept pot for her because it calmed her down. She said it kept her from wandering off, which, I don't know if that's true, but whatever. A friend and I stole some of Annie's pot. I took it to Marie, and I asked her to keep it for me. I really don't know what I was going to do with it. I didn't smoke pot, and I didn't want it except to impress this girl. But my friend and I took it, and I couldn't just throw it out. Anyway, I let slip to Marie that I knew where she kept her stash—in her boot. So, she took my baggie, but then she moved her stuff and put it in a jar under her mattress. She forgot Dad napped in her room on Sunday afternoons, and he felt the glass jar under the mattress when he lay on it. But if I could show you Dad's note, you'd know. You'd see. Except Marie stole the note."

She shook her head and stared at the paperwork. "Why are you trying to get your sister in trouble?"

I clenched and unclenched my fists beneath the table.

Breathe, Steven. Be cool with the fool.

"I'm not trying to get her in trouble. I'm telling you the truth. I didn't think Marie needed to go into a rehab, and I still don't. Maybe Julie Johnson needed help, but, you know, you can't just toss people into prison or prison substitutes because they do a little thing wrong here or there. Especially smoking a little grass. It's like...everybody does it." I knew this wasn't the greatest argument, but I did know plenty of people who smoked pot casually, infrequently, including my friend, Chris, and they seemed just fine.

"It doesn't make it right. If everybody started jumping off bridges, would you do it? This is why you need help, Steven. I wish you could see that."

My eggs and toast had to have gone cold by now. I picked up my fork and put it back down. I wasn't going to win this fight with my mom. Ever. "I'll never get through to you. You do what you want, Mom. Keep me from going to college for a year. But I'm not signing anything. I'm not agreeing to anything." I crossed my arms.

I was defiant.

But I was also finished.

Our front door creaked open.

"Hulllo!" Marie, dressed down in gym shorts and a cut-off Penrod's T-shirt, bounced down the hallway and into the kitchen, her sandals flapping on the laminated floor. "I figured you two would be up and at it by now." She plunked herself down beside my mom at the kitchen table. "Can you put a shirt on, Steven?" Marie asked. "Is that how you let him eat at the breakfast table, Mom? Half-naked?"

I sighed. "Screw off, Marie."

My sister laughed.

My mother cleared her throat. "Marie, we're in the middle of—"

"You should put those papers away." Marie tossed a folded-up piece of paper in front of my mother. "And read that. Do you still have the small baggie, mother? From the stuff you threw into the toilet last night."

My mother nodded.

"Okay, good. I figured you'd lock up the empty baggie in case you needed to show it to the police."

What was Marie doing? I eyeballed the piece of paper as my mother unfolded it, and it dawned on me what it was. My eyes widened. It couldn't be.

It is.

Is she?

Saving you. Marie is saving you.

No, it can't be.

It surely seems that way.

My mother smoothed the piece of paper on the table and then read it. Read it twice, it seemed, her eyes drifting back to the top and down again. Her forehead wrinkled as her pupils swooped back and forth across the page, absorbing the words. "What is this, Marie?"

My sister answered. "It's the real letter Dad wrote as he was dying, the one I stole from the shoebox under Steven's bed. By the way, you suck at hiding things, Steven."

"Steven told me you did that," my mother said in a hushed voice, her eyes never leaving the paper. "He was telling the truth."

Marie continued. "Yep. Steven took Dad's real note, and he faked a note that didn't mention Cher or me or the drugs. Look at the other letter, which I know you keep in your night table drawer; really look at it, and you'll see it's a phony, not Dad's handwriting but Steven's made to look like Dad's. This is the real letter, where Daddy admits what was eating at him." Marie wiped her eye. "What broke his heart."

"I don't understand." My mother's attention toggled between the looseleaf paper and Marie.

"You don't understand? Let me help. The drugs Dad found under my mattress almost four years ago were mine. Well, one of the bags was Steven's, even though he almost never got high. He was holding it for somebody. I blamed Cher to keep Steven and me out of trouble. And because you always believe everything I say, you agreed it was hers. It was an easier story for you to swallow, that our cousin, the outsider, was the bad girl. And Cher," my sister paused, leveling her eyes outside at the lake, "Cher had gotten an abortion, and I threatened her with it. I told her I would tell you about her abortion, and you would kick her out of the house. It was that, or she could just go into The Sprout for a couple of months. I was angry because Sal was the one who got her pregnant. And I thought she'd be fine. I figured, better Cher go in that hellhole than me or Steven. The Sprout would have broken little bro' into a million pieces—he wasn't as tough then as he is now, and he would have crumbled. Steven was just a dumb little baby, and I couldn't let him take the blame. I wasn't about to go in there. Cher was the easy answer. But that place was even worse than I thought. It crushed her. So, you killed her, Mother. Dad killed her, and he couldn't take it. I think that's why his heart gave out, between that and so many cigarettes. We all killed Cher." Marie made this claim so matter of fact. Like it was nothing. But I knew she harbored guilt over it. Maybe it made her feel better to spread the blame around. Or maybe she stated it because it was true. It was true, and none of us could take it back.

I wasn't sure what I was feeling, a chaotic mix of thoughts and emotions raced through me: relief, anger, guilt. And fear. Fear that my mother would put me into the rehab anyway despite hearing the truth. Fear that she was finished believing Marie and doing everything my sister told her to do.

"So that cocaine last night was yours. I should be calling the police on you, Marie. You're the one who needs help. I still have the empty baggie. With *residue*."

Marie broke into laughter. She laughed so hard she had to wipe her eyes. "Oh, my God! Not *residue*!" She waggled her fingers in the air. "Go check that baggie, Mother. Stick your finger inside and take a lick because you flushed powdered sugar down the toilet. But I suppose it helps the medicine go down, right? Sweet Jesus Christ above, you are something else, lady."

My mother's face registered a weird blend of enlightenment and confusion. "Your brother is lying like a druggie. He was smoking last night, I know it. I still can put him in—"

"God, when will you stop? Just stop, Mother. You have no proof Steven did anything wrong. If you put Steven in a rehab, I will personally yank him out myself on his birthday in four weeks, and he'll come live with me. And we'll somehow get him into college where he belongs, and he and I will never speak to you again."

Marie was speaking on my behalf, but whatever. I wasn't going to contradict her at this point, although I could never see myself doing that to my mom, not speaking to her again. But who knows? Who knows how I would feel after spending three-and-a-half weeks with Simon, Rebeccah, and their minions at the rehabilitation center formerly known as The Sprout?

"Why?" My mother's voice was so, so small. "Why would you do all this, Marie?"

"She did it to get back at me," I interjected. "I stole from Marie to pay Annie back, and so Marie finally got me back."

Marie grinned at me slyly. She nonchalantly gathered her mane of blonde hair into a ponytail and secured it with a light green scrunchy. After this, she patted my shoulder, snagged my fork, and took a bite of my eggs. "Ugh, they're cold." She swallowed her bite. "Maybe that was part of it, little bro, getting you back. But you know, that wasn't everything, or I wouldn't be here today. I had my reasons." She gave my mom a close-lipped, contented smile. My mom's face, again, had grown ashen.

It was never about you, Steven. Not mostly. Marie wanted to stick it to your mom.

Yes. I just figured that out.

"Gerald knew the drugs were yours, Marie." My mom stated my dad's name, which we barely uttered in our house anymore. She folded the looseleaf paper, slipped it into the front pocket of her slacks, and planted a steely gaze on my sister. "God is at work here. In all of this."

Marie scoffed. "Is She? Is She at work?"

"Don't blaspheme. God made you come here with this letter, Marie. He wants you to get help, Marie. Marie, you're a druggie, and you need help. Don't you see how all this fits together? It's not too late. I can change this paperwork for you. I've already spoken to the bank about another loan. We can make it work for you. We can do this together. For you."

Marie blew out hard, her breath a low whistle. "Wow." She stood and leaned over my mom, sticking a judgmental pointer finger a smidge from her nose. "Why don't you call the cops then? Tell the police I'm dealing pure-powdered sugar. In fact, I'm supplying all the bakers in

Little Havana. All their pastelitos are filled with my illegal sweet sugar."
Marie snorted and gathered the paperwork that sat in disarray in front
of my mother. She tapped the papers straight with each other, and with
a flourish, she tore them in half. She tossed the ripped papers into the
trash can under the sink. "Sorry, I'm leaving you here with her, Steven.
I gave you a scare, but that's all I ever wanted to do to you. You're not
a bad kid. I always protected you. I protected you more than you'll ever
know, but you betrayed me by stealing from me. Anyway, now we're
good."

"Gee, thanks. Are we good?"

Marie, hovering over the trash can, jabbed her pointer finger at our
mother again. "No rehab for him, Mother. Do you understand? You…"
I sensed she was holding back from calling our mom some choice
names. "You'll need Steven to take care of you in your old age. 'Cause I
sure won't."

My mother's lack of response, her posture, communicated
everything I needed to know. Marie had won me my freedom. She'd
swooped in like the calvary and saved me. But what she did was never
about me and her. It was about the bizarre love triangle formed among
my mother, Marie, and my mother's fabricated version of God. My
sister—whom my mother in some sense worshipped enough to
rationalize away every bad thing Marie did—wanted to jar my mother
out of her delusions and break her mindless faith. But all she really did
was cause my mom to replace one misconception with another. So, now
my mother knew the sad truth about Cher. About my dad. But the facts
would never break my mom's heart because she could slather her
religious fantasies on top of the pain and massage the truth so it fit
whatever theory of the day that she might create about how God had
worked His hand on our family.

Despite everything, I did not doubt God was often at work somehow, someway, in our lives. I truly believed God was with us, hovering or whatever, shaking their head in sorrow and joy, depending on the moment. But I simply didn't believe God was at work the way my mom thought. Unlike her, I left that mystery alone. And I could tell Marie felt the same as me. But even though my sister slammed the front door of our house victoriously, I knew she hadn't won entirely. Because there was no big win when it came to our mom. When you dealt with somebody who could summon the Father or the Holy Spirit's presence into every little event to fit their story, you would never win an argument.

The good news, though, was that I wouldn't be going to The Sprout—Straight and Narrow. Whatever.

I rose, cleaned off my plate, and placed it into the dishwasher. "I'm going to go to Marie's. She seems upset. I'll calm her down."

"Okay." My mom sat statuesque at the kitchen table.

"After that, I'm going to Chris's for Sunday dinner, okay?" I hadn't necessarily been planning to go to Chris's for dinner, although as I said it, it sounded like a good idea.

"Okay. Be careful. Come home early. It's a school night." She made this request as if none of this had happened. It was as if ten minutes ago she hadn't been prepared to stick me into a notorious drug rehabilitation center the next day. Tomorrow, I would go to school as usual down in Hollywood.

"By nine-thirty," she specified. "You'll explain to his mother that I made a mistake. I'm sure that smell on the patio was coming from somewhere else. Maybe the mechanic who lives two doors down. His patio. Let her know I'm sorry and that no marijuana was involved. It was a big misunderstanding."

Hell had frozen over. She admitted to making a mistake and said she was sorry. Maybe not an apology to me. Nor to Marie. Nor to Cher. But she admitted to making a mistake in accusing Chris. Okay then, good enough. "I will. I'm sure it's no big deal."

I was sure it wasn't. A big deal, that is.

I put on a T-shirt, slipped into my flip-flops, and drove to Marie's place. My sister answered the door and without uttering a word, let me into her apartment. The living room swam in a haze of spicy pot smoke. Blond surfer Rick, wearing only black and light-blue board shorts, his golden tanned body as buff as ever, hunched forward on an overstuffed couch, his lips around a gurgling bong on the coffee table in front of him. He blew out a thick stream of smoke, coughed once, and grinned. "Yo! Little bro! Come get a hit, Stevie!"

"I'm good, thanks."

"Okay, man. All good. Have some leftover tacos, bro. They're choice."

Marie waved me into the kitchen. We sat facing each other at her small, round Formica-topped table. "You want a taco?" she asked.

I chuckled at the absurdity of it all. "No, thanks." My stomach gurgled. I hadn't eaten more than a bite of the eggs and toast I'd made earlier. "Well, maybe."

She rose and produced two tacos from a plastic bin in her fridge. "Dos tacos. You want them microwaved or cold?"

"Uh, cold is okay, thanks."

"Okay, here let me put the shredded lettuce and tomato on them. And some sour cream." She placed a plate with the two loaded tacos in front of me, along with a jar of salsa, a spoon, and a bottle of tabasco sauce. "I'll get you some milk." She poured me a glass of milk and sat across from me.

"You ate?" I asked her.

233

"I did. Go ahead, eat." Marie slid a paper napkin toward me.

I spooned some salsa onto the taco, shook out some hot sauce on top of the salsa, and took a bite. "Mmm, really good." I wiped my mouth, chewed, and swallowed as she watched. "Thanks."

"Mmm, hmm."

"Two years ago, when I found coke under my bed and threw it in the lake, was that powdered sugar, too?"

She smirked but didn't answer. Her smirk said it all, though.

"Yeah, I figured. You really did a number on me, Marie."

"Good." She replied with a flat expression. Then, she said something unexpected. "I'm sorry I gave up Cher, Steven. I really am sorry. Okay? I know you need to hear that. I'm not going to tell you it's not partly your fault because we all played a part. We all did. But I am sorry I had to choose you and me over her. Sometimes there's nothing you can be but the bad guy. Or bad girl. It feels like I'm always the bad girl."

I chewed the taco as she poured out her heart to me. I swallowed again.

"That's bullshit, Marie. You didn't need to do all that to Mom. And it didn't matter anyway because Mom's going to believe what she wants to believe. She's not the real bad guy. And neither are you." I thought of Rebeccah Childs, the bone chiller. The bogeywoman. "The bad person is the person who does the real bad things and says they're doing something good."

"Hmm. One day, you'll understand, bro. You'll make a tough choice like I did, and you'll get it." As if in synchronicity with my thoughts, Marie mentioned the person I'd been thinking about. "Here's something else. That lady, Rebeccah, she really is headed to a rehab up in Pennsylvania. Near Philadelphia. I've got a friend on the inside of that place, and they told me she's been interviewing up north for a long time, and she finally landed a job. She's still at The Straight and Narrow, but she's leaving soon. Rats flee a sinking ship. That place is going down, and she probably made a fortune. I think she was a part owner with Howell."

"More lies?"

"It's true. One of my friends sells weed to one of their senior counselors. What a joke. Honest to God, it's true."

"You don't believe in God, Marie."

"I do believe in God. Do you, Steven?"

"Hmm. I guess? Not the way Mom does, but I do. Why are you telling me this?" How did she even know I cared about what happened to Rebeccah?

It's obvious, Steven. Marie knows you best—inside and out. She knows you better than I know you, and I can hear your thoughts.

Marie shrugged. "I thought you'd like to know. Information is powerful. It's why we spy on the Soviets."

"Okay. Are you happy I got what was coming to me?"

"I'm not happy. But, yeah, you got what was coming to you, and it wasn't that bad. Do you want a third taco? You ate those fast."

"Nah. I'm good."

Was I? Good?

"So, the lady that tortured our cousin is headed north."

"And you're headed to Miami in the fall, right?"

"Hmm. Yeah. Gonna come to my graduation?"

"Wouldn't miss it. Want some more milk? A chocolate chip cookie?"

"Why are you being so nice to me?"

"I've always been nice to you, Steven."

"Not true. You've acted mean to me because you can. You even said so."

Surfer Rick ambled into the room. "It's smoke-up Sunday," he murmured. "Gonna scarf down a taco." My sister swatted his taut backside as he passed her. "Don't touch the merchandise," he mumbled, rummaging through their fridge.

Marie swiveled in her chair and gave me a deadpan look. "Yes, Steven, I'm mean to you because I can." She folded her arms across her chest. "Do you want a chocolate chip cookie? It's not store-bought. I made them."

I nodded. "Sure, why not?"

"Rick, grab Steven a cookie, please. They're in a bin in the cabinet with the dinner plates."

"Your wish is my command," Rick replied, reaching into the cabinet.

She smirked. "See, that Steven? That, right there is the secret to life, little bro. My wish is *his* command." She winked at me, and I knew she was correct. Some people, like it or not, were always in charge, and Marie was one of those people. It's why my mother always believed her, always sided with her. It's why my father had acquiesced to her. It's why I would always bump heads with her.

But like Rob Sheldon once told me, I could be anything I wanted to be. And now I knew what I needed to do.

So, I grabbed the cookie, said thanks, and stood, my chair legs scraping her kitchen floor. I took a bite of the cookie. It was scrumptious, both salty and sweet and loaded with melted chocolate chips. Cookie in hand, I headed toward the front door of her apartment.

"Rude," she called after me. "Eating and running."

I opened her front door. "I've got somewhere I gotta go."

The Garbage Man

"What's up?"

"Is your dad here?"

Peter's tanned face remained impassive for a moment. Then he answered flatly, "What the fuck is wrong with you, man? We're not good enough for you, so you stop hanging with us. You rat me out. And now you wanna talk to my dad? He's busy, dickhead. He's not home."

A basketball game played on the television in their family room. The dark hair of his dad's head protruded from the back of a leather armchair. "Listen, man, he's right there in your family room. I can see him."

"So?"

"So, I only ratted you to Annie. It's not like I told any parents or the cops. And you kicked my ass—"

"I did kick your ass. Don't forget it." Peter's chest puffed out a couple of inches.

"And I let you into the theatre this summer. And I didn't say a word when you and Joey walked into *Risky Business* and *Vacation*."

"Gee, thanks."

237

"I need two seconds to ask your dad a question. Please."

"See, this is why nobody likes you, Stevie. You only come around when you need something."

"That's not true."

Well, maybe it's true for him, Joey, and Billy.

Shh, Shpresa.

Peter held the door open, but he stood silently in my way. As if he was taunting me.

"If you ever needed me, Peter, I would show up. We don't hang out, but I'd be there in a second to back you up."

That was the truth. I was loyal to a fault, sometimes even to people who didn't deserve it.

"What's it about? Did your little girlfriend get in trouble selling drugs?"

"She wasn't my girlfriend. And I haven't seen her in over a year," I lied. "She must have moved out of state. One question. I've got one innocent question for your dad."

Something changed in his eyes.

"Come in, douche." He waved me in. "I don't know why I'm helping you. Don't say anything stupid or illegal to him, huh? Watch your mouth. If you get me in trouble, I'll kick your ass again."

"Okay."

Peter's house was modest in size, like mine, but more tastefully appointed. A painting of a ship in troubled waters sat over the fireplace his father had built six years ago with imported stones from Italy that we kids had helped him carry in. In the painting, a man who looked like Jesus sat in the middle of the boat, so I assumed the other men around him must be the disciples. I stopped in front of the painting, examining it, as Peter bent and whispered into his dad's ear.

238

"You like this painting?" His father had sidled next to me. He was a large man, several inches taller than me, with a thick, boxy face permanently darkened by a five o'clock shadow. His near jet-black hair was slicked back. He wore, as usual, a bowling shirt, dark with a cream stripe on each side, and tan slacks. He smelled of mints and Old Spice aftershave and maybe a faint trace of cigar smoke.

I wanted to say the painting was new because I didn't recall seeing it in their family room. I hadn't been inside Peter's house in about two or so years, though, so I kept quiet. "It's...dynamic. The interplay of light and dark is intriguing."

He laughed. "Peter's right, you are loquacious." He laid a thick hand on my shoulder. "You know what that means? Loquacious?"

"Uh, yes, sir." I glanced around the house. When I walked in, Peter's mother had been busy in the attached kitchen, but she had not said hello to me, and now she was gone. Had she gone into the garage? Outside? Peter was gone too, maybe in his bedroom. It was Peter's dad and me alone—what I had wanted.

He pointed at the painting. "It's a small-scale reproduction. A famous artist, I won't say who, painted it for a friend of ours. It's called *The Storm on the Sea of Galilee*. The original is a much larger painting, a masterpiece by Rembrandt, and it hangs in the Gardner Museum up in Boston. Of course, you need to pay money to stare at it up there." He sniffed. "You in trouble? I thought you kept your nose clean, Stevie. Why do you want to speak with me?"

"I–is there somewhere more private we can talk? Out back?"

"We're alone here. What do you think I do for a living, Steven?"

"Uh, you own a concrete company. Maybe another garbage company or something up north. Sometimes Peter goes up to New York for part of the summer. But not where Joey goes. The island?"

"A cousin of ours has a house in the Hamptons. We go up every spring and summer for a couple of weeks. That's in New York. Long Island."

"Yeah. I knew that."

"But you're right, I *manage* a concrete company. And we manage a garbage company, too."

It must have been apparent in my eyes that I was wondering why Peter's family didn't live in a much bigger house on the intercoastal or down in fancy Coral Gables on the water.

"A man's gotta keep it simple, Steven. That's the secret to life. Before you ask me a question, I have a question for you. What happened between you and Peter and the rest of the boys? I know you and he got into a fight a year ago. But before that, you stopped coming around. Sorry about your father, by the way, God rest his soul." He crossed himself.

I swallowed hard, a thick vine growing in my throat, threatening to strangle me, choke off my words. "Thank you. It was my mom. She, uh…" I figured it would be easier to blame my judgmental mother than to explain the entire truth to him. It sort of was my mom.

He nodded. "Your mother is something else. A blonde Swedish, Polish queen. Like that gal from ABBA." He chuckled. "I can see how she would scare you. Did she tell you not to hang around my boy?"

Wait. Did he think my mom was a fox? Was my mom a fox? Billy had said something about her once. Well. Hmm. "No. It wasn't like that. I guess when I went to school down in Hollywood, I don't know, the guys and I grew apart. Living with my mom, it's tough to get out and stuff." Not entirely true, but close enough, although I sensed he could smell my mistruths.

"And now you want a favor from me." His eyes grew sharp. "But I run a garbage company. A concrete company. What could I do for you?" He scanned the painting as he spoke.

"I just want to ask you a question. Or tell you something I've been thinking about." I exhaled a shaky breath.

"Are you nervous?"

"Yes."

He guffawed and clapped me on the back. "Okay. You say what you've gotta say, and I'll listen. But be careful what you say. I'm not involved in anything illegal. And realize you'll always need to pay me back. If I do you a favor, whatever that is, how are you going to pay it back?"

"Money."

His Old Spice cologne wrapped its tendrils into the thick silence that followed. "You have money?"

"Not yet. But I will. I'll bartend after college if I need to. I'll make money."

"Confident."

"What I'm going to ask, uh, I'll keep it vague. It's just like, I might need a phone number of a guy who knows a guy. Someday."

"Explain."

So, I lowered my voice to beneath a whisper, and I explained what I needed from him, keeping my needs as nebulous as possible.

But he seemed to understand.

"Not today. Maybe not ever," I qualified.

He stared at me inexpressively with his Fred Flintstone-looking mug, and I nearly gave up my true intentions. "It's really about—"

"Whoa, whoa, whoa." He held up a massive hand. "That's enough. I don't want the end name."

"What?"

"You know what I mean, Steven. I don't want to know the object of your affections. The person at the end of this. I get the feeling you were about to tell me."

"Oh. Affections?"

"It's irony, Steven." A shrewd grin slipped onto his face. "You got some balls, kid, not hanging with my son for two years and coming here to work an angle."

"It's important to me."

"You should live your life, Steven. Peter always talks about how smart you are. How you were gonna make something of yourself. You got an academic scholarship to high school, and I bet you got an academic scholarship to college, right? Just like Peter got a baseball scholarship to Alabama."

Peter got a baseball scholarship to the University of Alabama? Wow. Good for him. I knew Peter was a star player on his high school team, but still. I tried not to let the surprise register on my face. "Yes, I'm going to Miami on a scholarship."

"Good school. Why come ask me for this kind of thing now? You're not even out of high school."

"I think my mom's going to move." Probably also true. But really, I figured strike while the iron was hot…or lukewarm.

"I'll think about it, Steven. You should go. And maybe I'll give you a number someday."

"Okay."

He walked me to the door. "Don't come back here. You're not friends with Peter. You made your choice. I'll help you, maybe, because he told me how you let him into the theatre this summer."

My eyes widened.

"He tells me many things. Like you ratted him to that girl."

I gulped. "I kept it between friends."

The man didn't respond to that.

I shifted my feet. "I never told any parents or anybody else."

"I know. But you shouldn't have said anything. We should be living here for a while, Steven. One phone call away. See you later, son. *Buona fortuna.* Good luck." The giant in the silky bowling shirt nearly shoved me out his front door, and it slammed on my butt. I stood on his stoop, wondering if I'd accomplished anything with this visit. Wondering if I'd feel the same when it came time to make the call.

Peter's house sat five houses down from mine on the cul-de-sac. I had parked my car at my house and walked down to his place, so I headed back home on foot. I figured I'd sneak into my house, avoiding my mother, and call Chris to see if his mom was making lasagna for dinner. She would be making her world-famous lasagna because it was Sunday. I'd be welcome, even if she thought we'd been smoking grass on my patio. Some people were cool, and you could just tell they'd forgive you and take things in stride.

Forgiveness. Taking things in stride. I wasn't there yet.

Not by a long shot.

You're going to have a good life, Shpresa butted in on my thoughts as I walked toward the cul-de-sac circle, headed toward my house. *You'll go to college. Maybe attend graduate school. Get a good job and have a nice family. You'll leave Florida. Don't waste your good life, Steven. Let it go. Forgive.*

A happy life? I asked her. *Are you saying I'll have a happy life, Shpresa? Because what's been happy so far? What's happy about all this?*

I was soaring now. I had been folded into a paper airplane, formed from a looseleaf note written by my father and launched by fate, gliding toward the pavement. Would I skid lightly and come to rest on a nearby sidewalk? Or would I break open, the guilt laced within the paper's words turning me solid and oh so fragile like bones? Would I plummet to my destiny, my bleached-white bones cracking open under the searing South Florida sun? Everybody always wanted to impart the secret of life to me, but that was the secret to life, wasn't it? We soar, and we fall, and we crash. We're light as a feather, and then disaster strikes, and we gain mass and break. We walk around life giving the appearance that we're whole when really our pieces, our shards, have been scattered across the dirty pavement. Paper airplane, broken bones. God doesn't need to play a part in all that.

How could I ever be happy, Shpresa? After all that's happened?

I said you'll have a good life, Steven. I didn't say you'll be happy. It might be too late for that. Don't push your luck.

A good life, Shpresa? I suppose I'll take it.

I wondered what a good life would entail. I had no point of reference, but the only person that came to mind was Annie LeFevre. A warm feeling of love coursed through me as I pictured her. A good life would require love. So, maybe a good life would mean finding and marrying somebody who cared about me and whom I cared about. Someone like Analynn, although I would never marry her—that was not going to happen. It got me pondering, now that Annie lived in Davie, would she ever buy a horse? I sure hoped she would.

Ideas of marriage skittered out of my mind, and I pictured my friend, Analynn, fully transformed once more, this time from a new-wave girl into a cowgirl wearing brown leather boots and a broad-brimmed hat. She rode a light brown female horse through a broad, grassy field in Davie, a tiny white butterfly fluttering in front of her steed. The late afternoon sunlight shone upon my first love's tanned face as the horse's hooves clopped gently down the path, kicking up dust. My cowgirl Annie steered her mare toward the setting sun.

As the sky turned pink, the sun a blood-red plum hanging in the mist, my darling Analynn headed home and thought of me. She wondered how I was doing.

That was my last thought before I went inside.

1992

Epilogue

Remembering the Most Horrible Thing

"You don't drink?" She nodded at my diet soda.

Finally, she sat beside me at the bar. Finally. Fourth time was a charm!

She caught me gripping the thick burger in both hands, the sandwich midway between my open mouth and the dinner plate on the glossy bar top. I placed the cheeseburger back on the plate and considered her. Her brown hair was slicked back from her forehead with blonde highlights running front to back, the short hairdo curling around the bottom of her neck. She seemed to be imitating the hairdo actress Sharon Stone sported in *Basic Instinct*, a movie that had debuted earlier in the year. Faint wrinkles played around the corners of her brown eyes as she smiled.

I smirked at her question. "I've got class tomorrow. I'm studying tonight, so, no alcohol for me tonight."

In response, she mimicked my expression. Was she flirting with me? Yes, maybe so. "You're a baby. How did they even let you in here? You must be like twenty, right?"

"I'm a third-year grad student at Temple. What's that you're drinking, bourbon?" I eyed her drink.

At the other end of the bar, Florence, her curly dark hair teased high above her head, served a couple of off-shift hospital employees. Florence was the bar manager and my girlfriend. She tossed me a sideways glance, like she was wondering what the heck I was doing. I winked at her with my right eye, so the woman, sitting to my left, wouldn't see it.

The woman scrunched her nose. "Bourbon? No. I'm drinking a Black Russian on the rocks."

"Hmm. Vodka and Kahlua." I took a bite of my burger. It was, as usual, superb. The cozy, three-story bar, *Birds 33*—named after the year, 1933, when the Philadelphia Eagles American football team was formed—was sandwiched between two brownstones and sat across Eleventh Street from Thomas Jefferson Hospital; it made the best cheeseburger in the city. Juicy and fat. Premium beef, flame broiled. Dripping.

"Good burger," she asked rhetorically, sipping her drink. "How old *are* you?"

She was fixated on my age. My youth, perhaps. That didn't surprise me. I held up a finger while I chewed and swallowed. "Old enough to know better." Where did that stupid line come from? "Where are you from?" I quickly asked her in follow-up.

Her eyes narrowed slightly.

Easy, Steve. Easy.

"Cincinnati, Ohio mostly. My father was an Army chaplain, so we moved around. You?"

"South Florida." Was there a flash of something in her eyes? Maybe. "Miami. I grew up near the Golden Glades interchange. I'm Steven. Steven Rankin."

She sipped at her dark drink. "What do you study?"

I leaned in. "I'm getting a Masters of Fine Arts in European Classic Literature at Penn." Another lie. I was in my third year of a four-year doctoral program in Social Psychology at Temple University. Social psychologists studied and analyzed data. At one time, I thought I wanted to study literature, but lately, I preferred the cold comfort of data.

"Hmm. Fine Arts. Sounds liberal. What exactly are you studying now?" She continued to sip her drink.

Thank you for the opening.

"The Count of Monte Cristo. By Dumas. Know it?"

She shook her head. "Heard of it, I guess."

"You haven't told me your name. Wait, let me guess, something with an S. Sharon? Like Sharon Stone."

She snorted as if I'd embarrassed her slightly. "No."

"So? What then?" I tilted my head down and toward her.

She shrugged. Let her be mysterious. All the better.

"What are you looking for?" I asked her. "A nice-looking woman drinking all by yourself?" I didn't mean for my comment to sound so sexist and cheesy, so much like a come-on, but it did. Still, I didn't regret asking it.

Her neck grew splotchy, a flush above her collarbones. Excitement? "You must be fifteen years younger than me. Am I right?"

"I'm going on twenty-six."

And you're pushing forty. Maybe thirty-eight or thirty-nine. So, let's say it's a fourteen-year difference.

I didn't ask her age. It would have been rude.

250

She blinked a little more rapidly. "So, what's the book you're studying about?"

Really? She never read *The Count of Monte Cristo* or even heard about it? "It's about a guy who makes his life revolve around the single most horrible thing that happened to him. It's what any good story is about: revenge."

Her stare grew hotter. "Is that true? Are all good stories about revenge? That's only one aspect of human life."

Aah, here she was, emerging from her slumber. Her eyes sharper, her lips set. Her mind was tuned to my every nuanced comment and question. I needed to be careful. Precise in my language. I leaned toward her, my chin on my shoulder conspiratorially. "About thirty seconds from now, scratch your back and look over your left shoulder at the guys sitting in the booth behind you."

She waited, then did as I said, and I took the opportunity to wolf down another bite of my burger. As I chewed, Florence made her way back to us. "You okay, babe?"

Florence called me babe to claim me as hers. I didn't mind. "Mmm, hmm," I nodded at her, and she walked away.

The woman had turned back to me. "Okay, I looked at them. Hey, what's with you and the bartender?"

She was perceptive, I'd give her that. "She's my girlf—we're dating."

"And you're coming on to *me*?"

"Was I?" I widened my eyes, trying to seem shocked.

She whispered. "So, what about those guys? They look like your standard-issue South Philly goombas."

She's crude in her thinking. Racist. Like some of those fascists from my neighborhood.

"The guy with the gray news cap on, Phil Benedetto, he knows about revenge. When Phil was younger, some guy from his neighborhood did his sister wrong. He found out where the guy moved to near Pittsburgh, and he followed him there, even enrolled at the University of Pittsburgh. He created this whole new life in a very specific city just to plan revenge. People do that, create new lives for themselves. Phil waited eight long years. Then…" I wagged my head from side to side as if I couldn't tell the rest of the story without revealing a major crime.

Her eyes narrowed. "You hang out with *those* guys? You look more like a white-bread Michael J. Fox than a South Philly guy." She squinted at me. "You look familiar."

She wasn't the first person to tell me I looked like the actor. "Who you calling white bread? Besides, I'm taller than Michael J. Fox." I stabbed her with a knowing side eye, and she laughed. "Maybe you've seen me here before. Or maybe I've got one of those faces." *I come here all the time. You, on the other hand, have come here three times in the last few weeks, at least that I know.*

"Touché. Yeah. You're built better than Michael J. Fox, too," she mumbled, eyeing my shoulders. She swigged her drink and raised her hand to summon Florence, who dutifully refilled her Black Russian. "I come across a lot of people in my job. What I do."

I was about to ask her about her job when we were interrupted. "Yo, Stevie! You talkin' shit about us over there?" Phil's gravelly voice rang across the narrow restaurant.

Darn. Why did Phil have to call me, Stevie? I swung around. "What are you gonna do about it?" I shouted back mockingly, but with a smile, and both hard-looking guys in the booth laughed along with me. They raised their glasses. I raised mine. The woman raised hers. We shouted 'Salud' and drank, after which I faced the mirror behind the bar. One thing I'll say about growing up where I did, I could assimilate, get along with anybody. And I didn't judge people by where they came from. People could surprise you if you gave them a chance.

"You're bold, talking to them like that." She sipped her drink, her cheeks reddening. She was feeling the effects of her second drink. She wasn't a big woman, indeed rather thin. Not larger than life after all. After all this time.

"We play pool together upstairs. Hang out some. They're good guys. So, what did you do? I mean, what do you do for a living?"

She didn't notice my gaffe. "I used to be a nurse." She offered this lie flawlessly as she sucked down her second drink. "I'm retired."

"Funny. You're so young. Living on an inheritance?" I joked.

"Yes. Something like that," she replied flatly.

"Really? What do you do with your time, watch movies all day?"

"Sure. That's it. No, I live around the corner. I do a little of this and a little of that to keep busy. I like it here, but I might move somewhere warmer soon. Maybe LA. I like the beach."

I know you do. Sounds dreamy. Will you make it to the warm beach? Who knows?

"Speaking of beaches, I just watched *Silence of the Lambs* on video. Have you seen it?" I asked.

"Uh, yes. I've seen it. What's that got to do with beaches?" She nodded at Florence and pointed at the lonely ice cubes in her glass. Time for a second refill. She was drinking faster now. Good.

"In the movie, the bad guy stalks his nemesis. That scene was shot in Bimini you know. It's down near the Bahamas. My buddy Ty Sweets from college, his family owns a hotel in Bimini right up that road from where that scene was shot. I've been there."

Florence, wearing a perturbed expression, poured the woman a third Black Russian. "What kind of nonsense are you talking over here, Steven?"

I shrugged. "Just talking movies and books." I sniffed. "Things we like to do for fun."

"What's he going to do, take advantage of me?" The woman took a sip of her fresh drink and grinned at my latest girlfriend.

Her inappropriate joke bounced ineffectively off Florence, who half-rolled her eyes at me, stung my new pal with a sharp glance, and departed to serve somebody down the bar.

"Uh, oh. I don't think your little girlfriend likes me." She sounded tipsy.

"Probably not, but we're just talking. Be careful, though. Florence isn't someone to be messed with."

"Neither am I." The woman leaned into me, her shoulder brushing my shoulder. Her perfume reeked of lavender, and I swallowed a gag. "If you want to walk me to my apartment later, you can. I could use an escort."

There it was.

I whispered back, "Maybe next time, sorry. I really do have a test tomorrow." In another world, with another person, I might have. Since I hit my mid-twenties, I found women in their thirties more interesting than those in their twenties. Florence, a no-nonsense girl from Roxborough, was the first woman my age I'd dated since I'd arrived in Philly three years earlier.

"Right. You have a test. You said that." The woman straightened herself, mild embarrassment creeping across her face. "So, in the book you're studying, what happens at the end?"

"You never read it? Well, let's just say he lives his life."

"Is he happy?"

"Probably not. But he has a good life, I bet. Are *you* happy?"

She appraised me with dead eyes, her lids droopy under the haze of the alcohol she'd been swigging. I really, truly, looked at her—saw her—and an unexpected wave of nausea washed over me, a Pavlovian response. The next thing she said was unexpected, but, considering, it wasn't that shocking: "I'm happy because my Lord Jesus loves me. Even if I'm a sinner."

There you are. Poking out of your shell.

I tried to look surprised. "Hmm. Understood."

I faced the bar mirror again, my face rugged under three-day stubble. Look what I had become, thicker, callused, even at twenty-five. I whistled a tune, and its piercing melody sliced like a glowing knife through "Personal Jesus," the Depeche Mode song burbling from the bar's speakers. Her drink halted halfway to her mouth, rocks glass quivering in mid-air. I continued whistling. She placed her drink on her bar napkin, traced her fingertip around the lowball glass's rim. Deep in thought.

I stopped whistling. "I'm whistling "What Child is This?" It's a Christmas carol set to the tune of "Greensleeves," which is a traditional English folk song. Do you know it?"

"Oh. Yes, of course." Her voice was thin. Did she know who I was? At this point, it didn't matter.

"Sounds like "Greensleeves," though, right?"

She didn't answer. "Are you a Christian?" she queried.

"Uh-huh, Catholic." At least, I went to Catholic high school for four years, so I could fake it. "All honor to almighty God, who in his great power can do infinitely more within us than we could ask or imagine." I knew I'd mangled the verse even worse than I had when I was a fourteen-year-old child, a dove, speaking to this woman for the first time.

She stared at me with a super-hot intensity now, and she forced a chuckle. "Ephesians. But that's not quite the verse."

We were playing that kids' game, warmer-colder, and she was burning hot, about to get singed, but she wasn't quite aware of it yet. "Yeah, I don't remember the verse exactly. But I suppose my version is good enough for today."

Was that what she said to me in her tiny, wood-paneled office?

Something behind her eyes clicked, and the color drained from her face. She swallowed hard, and I chomped into my burger, a stream of warm gray-burgundy meat juice dripping down the side of my hand. "So delicious," I muttered out the side of my mouth. I wiped away the runoff with a white paper napkin.

Scrub the stain away.

Blood sloshing over the bathtub.

Baptized in my cousin Cher's crimson innocence.

I'd really come into my own, embraced the searing pain of my childhood.

The woman, her eyes straight ahead, tossed a twenty-dollar bill onto the bar. She gathered her things, clutching her purse as if I might steal it. She stumbled a bit as she climbed off her stool, the effects of the alcohol or a sign of distress. "Nice meeting you, uh, Steve," she muttered, still looking to the side of me. Averting her eyes.

She hurried toward the bar's front door, edging past other customers, forging her escape. "Nice meeting you too, Rebeccah!" I shouted after her, my voice burying the lyrics of Kurt Cobain, who growled the song "Polly" rough and low over the bar's speakers.

She clutched the handle of the bar's front door and twisted her head at the sound of her name. Her face had gone deathly pale, eyes large within her bloodless visage. That terrified look was all I needed. Her expression, her fear, would need to last me the rest of my life. Or haunt me the rest of my life. Or both.

This is for Cher.

She flew from the bar.

I rotated on my stool and popped my head up, peering over the crowd toward the back of the narrow pub. I nodded at the thin, dark-bearded man who sat alone in a booth near the kitchen. His eyes met mine, but he didn't nod back. The nameless guy, who was known by another guy but not by me, slid out of the booth. He fastidiously buttoned his navy pea coat around his slender frame. He wormed his way to the front of the bar and followed the woman out the door.

One name was all I needed. I did the rest, made the phone calls.

It's cold outside. And I am so cold inside. I am so cold and dark now.

It was a lot of money you spent on him, Steven. All that bartending money from your year off. You could have put that money toward a down payment on a house.

Shpresa hadn't spoken to me for three years, not since I'd crossed from South Carolina into North Carolina at the South of the Border rest area during my move to Philadelphia. This is what she decided to say to me after three years of silence, that I could manage my money better?

I made a boatload of money bartending in my year off between college and grad school, Shpresa. I can spend it how I like. And I can always make more. I'm going to have a good life after all, right? That's what you told me when I made that deal with Peter's dad.

My friend did not respond.

You've got something you want to say to me, Shpresa? You want to tell me I'm a horrible person? Tell me to run after him and put a stop to it? Or go easier and merely scare her like Marie scared me in '84? I only want this woman

257

to remember me the way I remember her. That's all. Is that too much to ask? I want to be her personal monster.

Florence appeared in front of me. "Refill on your soda, babe?" I bobbed my head yes and smiled at her. She rolled her eyes again. "That lady was something, coming on to you right in front of me. Not that you were discouraging her." Her eyes narrowed.

"Thanks for the refill. I was playing along. She was a lousy drunk, that's all."

"Maybe," she answered, irritation dancing in her eyes. "Maybe *you* could use a drink, Steve." She was right. Blunt Florence Bernstein was a tough girl; she reminded me of my old friend Annie in her demeanor and frankness, if not necessarily her accent or physical appearance. No matter what happened between us, Florence, like Annie, would be okay.

My relationship with Florence wouldn't last more than another month, but at that point, I didn't know the ignominious fate of our short-lived fling. Florence would represent one in a string of relationship failures over the next year or two. Until I succeeded and found someone right for me.

We fail, and we fail, and we fail. And sometimes we get lucky.

I paid my bill, and Florence told me she'd swing by my place later.

As I headed toward the bar's front door, I pictured myself a few minutes in the future, strolling up Eleventh Street toward my apartment on Pine. I would follow the tracks, the sickly lavender scent, of the woman who, moments before, had staggered to her spacious Spruce Street dwelling—the condominium with a back door lock that, to my understanding, was easy to pick. I'd pass her house.

The thin, bearded man from the back of the bar would not have passed by. He would be lurking in a dark corner of her kitchen as she fumbled to chain-lock her back door from the inside. As she flipped a light switch, once, twice, with no effect because her power had been turned off. She would gasp and drop her keys when he stepped out of the shadows and into her life.

Like she had stepped into my life. Stepped into Cher's life. Stepped into Julie's life.

How much suffering had this woman caused?

Predator turned prey.

It is cold and dark outside. I can be anything I will myself to be, and I am cold and dark. I am the sum of the frigid nothingness that has been shoved inside of me like murky stuffing into a dead bird's hollowed guts. I am the head scarecrow in charge now.

Maybe, after I whistled past Rebeccah's brownstone and reached the rolled-up sofa bed in my studio apartment, I would make believe I was sitting alone at a hotel bar in North Bimini. Like at The Compleat Angler where Ernest Hemingway wrote *To Have and Have Not*. I'd put on a soft rock CD and play "You Light Up My Life" by Debby Boone. I would crack open a Jamaican Red Stripe beer, and I'd drink it by myself in celebration before Florence showed up. *Red Stripe.* Or I'd give Marie a holler, my annual call to check in with my sister, although she, as always, would be doing fine. Marie was in charge, too, and she was always fine. And I was fine, too. *Red Stripe.* We fail, and we fail, and we fail. And then, on a blue moon, we get it right. And then we fail some more. Then, we win. *Red Stripe.*

Are you sure there's nothing you want to say to me, Shpresa? About what I've done. All I've done. About what's happening to Rebeccah now? About Cher? About my dad? About God? Don't you know Him where you live? Is God there? Does He or She forgive me for what I've done? What I'll do?

No, I have nothing to say. I'm going away, Steven. For a while. I'll see you much, much later.

Okay. Farewell, good friend. I'll see you on the other side.

Farewell, Steven.

A shiver crept up my arms. This was it for my buddy and me.

And Shpresa was true to her word. I didn't hear from her again for a long time, not until the very end.

Acknowledgements

First things first, I must thank my number one reader, my wife, Sheri Shifman. Her support goes beyond her incisive critiques and helpful suggestions, which made this story better. Without Sheri's unfailing love and encouragement, I could not have written this novel.

I also owe a debt of gratitude to my other readers, including Teresa Garcia, Paul Georgulis, John Merkle, Katy Nicholas, Barry Litherland, Steven Stern, and Jeanine Waldron. I'm grateful to my children, Eric and Lexi, who, though grown, bring a deep sense of purpose to my life, and from whom I am always learning.

Thank you to the folks at Between the Lines Publishing, including Siân Hyleg for her support, Abby Macenka and Penny Dowden for their tremendously helpful editing, and Morgan Bliadd for designing a powerful cover. I appreciate the team's belief in my work and their efforts to make it shine. Finally, I'm oddly grateful for some of the painful childhood memories that inspired this story.

R.B. Shifman is an author and market research contractor. Raised in South Florida, he resides near Doylestown, Pennsylvania with his wife. He writes young adult and middle grade novels across various genres—drama, fantasy, and horror. His weird fiction short story, "Mayo Monday," written as Richard Shifman and suitable for all ages, headlined Cosmic Horror Monthly magazine in October 2023. He has two grown children.

www.ingramcontent.com/pod-product-compliance
Lightning Source LLC
Chambersburg PA
CBHW011228120626
46549CB00008B/3183

* 9 7 8 1 9 6 5 0 5 9 2 6 5 *